PRAISE FOR

Family Entrepreneur

"Author Fred Dawkins has penned another winner with *Family Entrepreneur*. The third-party narrative style of storytelling allows for a variety of opinions to be put forward while maintaining an entertaining read. Chocked full of real-life scenarios and challenges that face every business, this book will engage all entrepreneurs from every generation, whether in a family business or not."

— David Wojcik, host and executive producer, BiZ TV Canada.

"Fred Dawkins sure can tell a story.... With *Family Entrepreneur* he gives us a great story and a pleasant read. He provides wisdom, comfort, and learning about entrepreneurship from a family enterprise point of view.... If you are part of a family enterprise, here's a chance to learn from Fred, an accomplished family entrepreneur, and make your life much more effective and rewarding."

— Brendan Calder, entrepreneur in residence and adjunct professor, GettingItDone, Rotman School of Management at the University of Toronto.

"Fred's book is thought-provoking and highly entertaining while being truly insightful. Readers are challenged on their own beliefs and characteristics regarding entrepreneurship, mentors, career, and family. At times I was laughing and other times intrigued by the business concepts subtlety being offered. It is full of rich ideas on how to develop and maintain a how to build a business the right wa caused others to stumble. As a ser coach I highly recommend Fred's *Family Entrepreneur* for those in business or thinking about starting one."

— Bill Simmel, CEO and founder, Phoenix ONE Sales, Marketing, Management + Communications Inc.

"In his second book, *Family Entrepreneur*, Fred Dawkins uses the same intimate discussion format that made his first book, *Everyday Entrepreneur*, so informative and such a great text for seminars. Fred's experiences as a successful family entrepreneur form the basis of real-life discussion for concepts such as funding through leadership and the pitfalls and opportunities of personal issues, entitlement, rewards, and succession that have special significance in a family setting.… Whether a beginner, well into an entrepreneurial venture, or a professor of business, this book is a must. It's great stuff."

— Dr. Freeman McEwen, dean emeritus, University of Guelph.

"Reading Fred Dawkins's book is like having an experienced business coach who's already walked down the same road you're traveling, right there with you. While reading this book you're bound to sigh with relief as he examines all the mildly crazy things we do as family entrepreneurs. (We are not alone!) You'll raise your eyebrows, smack yourself on the forehead, and underline text reflecting his simple solutions and powerful observations, and you'll feel a surge of motivation as you put them into play immediately. So accurate are his examples of family business dynamics that you'll feel such a familiarity you'll swear he's been reading your email. Written in a storybook format that's enjoyably easy to read, you'll want to take this book along with you on your next vacation. I have a hunch it's going to be a book I return to and recommend on a very regular basis."

— Sherri J. Griffin, training and development professional.

"... Focusing on family business and family dynamics, the *Family Entrepreneur* will give you the courage to tackle your own situation. Family relationships are complicated in the best of circumstances, and running a company means constantly adapting to changing environments. Dawkins provides sage advice for anyone in a family business, emphasizing how important it is to face the issues head-on as rationally as you can and not to allow emotion to dominate the conversation.... The valuable insights will guide you no matter where you are on the entrepreneurial timetable."

— Dr. Elizabeth A. Stone, dean, Ontario Veterinary College (OVC), University of Guelph.

"In the fast-paced age of corporations and global multi-billion dollar industries, *Family Entrepreneur* is a riveting road map for all readers, regardless of their desire to become an entrepreneur.... Effective and cleverly narrated through the eyes of a young female entrepreneur, *Family Entrepreneur* showcases the challenges, rewards, and opportunities within life and family business from varying timelines. It's easy to find one's self and relate to the characters throughout the book. It reads like a novel, but is a sneaky and fun way of teaching the tools of the trade of family entrepreneurship."

— Maryam Latifpoor-Keparoutis, senior development manager, College of Physical & Engineering Science (CPES), University of Guelph.

"Utilizing his exemplary storytelling skills, Fred Dawkins has written an excellent book about entrepreneurship in a family setting environment.... He cleverly exposes how frequently family members butt heads during the running of a family business and how difficult it can be to resolve differences among family members. If you're a small business or entrepreneur working with your family in your business, I would highly recommend that you read *Family Entrepreneur*. It will provide you with valuable insights on how you might be better able to deal with the challenges in running a 'family' business."

"Fred Dawkins does it again with his second book in the Entrepreneurial Edge series. *Family Entrepreneur* presents us with yet another set of entrepreneurial everymans (and women) amongst whom every reader can find a kindred soul. Learning through these characters feels like private advice shared over coffee with a dear friend. It's the kind of advice that sticks with you and the kind of book you will return to. As an entrepreneur currently working alongside family, this is a book I will share with everyone on our team, be they related or not."

"Fred Dawkins sure can tell a story. I really enjoyed his previous one: *Everyday Entrepreneur.* Again with *Family Entrepreneur* he gives us a great story and a pleasant read. He provides wisdom, comfort, and learning about entrepreneurship from a family enterprise point of view. I kept thinking of those I know in that situation that would have benefited from reading it earlier in their life. If you are part of a family enterprise, here's a chance to learn from Fred, an accomplished family entrepreneur, and make your life much more effective and rewarding."

THE ENTREPRENEURIAL EDGE

FAMILY
Entrepreneur
EASIER SAID THAN DONE

Fred Dawkins

DUNDURN
TORONTO

Editor: Jennifer McKnight
Design: Laura Boyle
Cover Design: Laura Boyle
Cover Image: © alexskopje/ iStockphoto.com
Printer: Webcom

Library and Archives Canada Cataloguing in Publication

Dawkins, Fred, 1945-, author
    Family entrepreneur : easier said than done / Fred Dawkins.

(The entrepreneurial edge)
Issued in print and electronic formats.

ISBN 978-1-4597-2275-0 (pbk.).--ISBN 978-1-4597-2276-7 (pdf).-- ISBN 978-1-4597-2277-4 (epub)

1. Family-owned business enterprises. 2. Entrepreneurship. 3. Success in business. I. Title. II. Series: Entrepreneurial edge (Series)

HD62.25.D39 2014   658'.045   C2014-905034-8
                                           C2014-905035-6

1 2 3 4 5   18 17 16 15 14

 Conseil des Arts du Canada / Canada Council for the Arts  Canada  ONTARIO ARTS COUNCIL CONSEIL DES ARTS DE L'ONTARIO an Ontario government agency un organisme du gouvernement de l'Ontario

We acknowledge the support of the **Canada Council for the Arts** and the **Ontario Arts Council** for our publishing program. We also acknowledge the financial support of the **Government of Canada** through the **Canada Book Fund** and **Livres Canada Books**, and the **Government of Ontario** through the **Ontario Book Publishing Tax Credit** and the **Ontario Media Development Corporation**.

Care has been taken to trace the ownership of copyright material used in this book. The author and the publisher welcome any information enabling them to rectify any references or credits in subsequent editions.

J. Kirk Howard, President

The publisher is not responsible for websites or their content unless they are owned by the publisher.

Printed and bound in Canada.

VISIT US AT
Dundurn.com | @dundurnpress | Facebook.com/dundurnpress | Pinterest.com/dundurnpress

DUNDURN
3 Church Street, Suite 500
Toronto, Ontario, Canada
M5E 1M2

Family bonds have a great hold on us all. Loyalty to family members can become an obsession, a step away from delusion. Some of us are determined to break that hold, others choose to ignore it. In the end most of us embrace it. When I was young, a wise man once told me "expect nothing from your children or your siblings and you won't be disappointed." At the time this seemed cynical, but as life evolved it became clear that we cannot plan the lives of our children. Love from a parent is unconditionally given for life; love from a child is eroded by the search for independence and the diversions of building a new life. Sibling relationships are complicated, immersed in issues that most of us ignore, like birth order, misunderstood jealousy, and subtle competitions. Family bonds demand loyalty and support, fostered by duty, while often breeding entitlement and abuse, routed in sibling rivalry. There are few elements of life so frustrating or so rewarding. With that in mind, this book is dedicated to families, in general, and mine in particular. A life worth living finds balance and family is the solid foundation to build on. I am grateful for the relationships I've enjoyed with all of my family, both personal and business, from grandparents to grandchildren. My career and my life would be inconsequential without you.

"If you cannot get rid of the family skeleton, you may as well make it dance."

— George Bernard Shaw

CONTENTS

PREFACE

There has been a rush toward entrepreneurship over the past ten years, particularly since the onslaught of the Great Recession in 2008. Since that time virtually every college and university has added courses on the subject. Academics and governments around the world are scrambling to find effective ways to teach the associated skills and to create ecosystems that support the development of entrepreneurship.

There are good reasons for this new approach. The two most dominant influences in the world today are globalization and technology. Globalization is increasing the supply of available labour. Through mechanization and innovation, technology is reducing the demand for labour. Both of these trends are putting downward pressure on real wages rates, the burden of which is greater in the established western economies. As consumption increases in developing economies, there will be an increase in demand for labour, but much of this will benefit workers in those other economies. Together globalization and technology guarantee that the one constant in our lives is, and will continue to be, rapid change. To embrace change, all of us must become more adaptable and resilient, which are key characteristics for entrepreneurs. The status quo is constantly under attack, putting great value on those who disrupt and challenge current practice. Disruption is the backbone of entrepreneurship.

In the West, the most important skill an individual can develop is the ability to create and manage their own career. Becoming an entrepreneur allows you to keep yourself employed and capture the value added for whatever good or service you provide. It can also create jobs and opportunities for others. If running your own business is not for you, becoming entrepreneurial and making strategic employment decisions will increase the value of your labour and provide upward mobility. In the simplest terms, we all must become more entrepreneurial.

ACKNOWLEDGEMENTS

I owe a great deal of gratitude to Professor Ajay Agrawal of the Rotman School at the University of Toronto for seeing merit in the first book in this series, *Everyday Entrepreneur.* Also to Jesse Rogers, director of the Creative Destruction Lab, which was founded by Ajay. Both have encouraged me to develop my mentorship of aspiring entrepreneurs and in doing so have introduced me to a wide range of extremely talented young people who will have a very significant impact on Canada over the next fifty years and more. Ajay is committed to building and enhancing an ecosystem that will keep the best and most brilliant people that we produce active and productive right here. In a world competing for talent this is a critical goal. Ajay is one of the most entrepreneurial people that I know, which means that he is capable of great things. Nothing that he accomplishes will surprise me and his accomplishments have been and will continue to be many.

The most important person for me to acknowledge is my wife, Karin, for her love and support. For almost fifty years she has had to absorb daily conversations that include a never-ending stream of ideas and projects. She is my first sounding board and the anchor that keeps me grounded. At least we both agree that it has never been boring.

INTRODUCTION

The Family Brand

The butcher, the baker, the candlestick maker — rhyming words from an old nursery rhyme and all three were family businesses, not to mention the tailor, the lawyer, the publican, and of course the farmer. Pre-industrial revolution apprenticeships led most to follow in the footsteps of dear old dad. That's why we have surnames like Archer, Barber, Brewer, Carpenter, Cooper, Farmer, Fisher, Gardner, Hunter, Mason, Miller, Smith, Taylor, and Tanner, to name but a few. Opportunity was pretty much limited to following the family trade, if you were lucky enough to have one. The industrial revolution changed that dramatically, breaking patterns that had gone on for generations by creating new jobs, including owners and managers, in much larger entities. Manufacturing also added great scope for bringing family members into the fold if you happened to own a factory. Towns sprung up around industry, often located in areas that were accessible to the raw materials or water that would be needed. The company town evolved as people located in these same areas to find work. In each case the company became the principal employer and supplemented the established trades as the convenient sources of work. Local businesses have traditionally been a family affair.

Of course, some of those local businesses became nationally and even internationally known. Families provided the original business incubators and formed the foundation that allowed many to pursue the American dream, focused on upward mobility. Extended family members were the original "crowd" that provided funding. Family units invented "bootstrapping" before anyone had a term for it. Family networks offered the main foundation for startups, especially once public education became available. Educate one son, help him start a business, and the entire family could be lifted out of poverty. Unconditional family support provided the principal entrée to entrepreneurship long before any of us knew what an entrepreneur was. To own your own business was liberating; to staff it with family was convenient and rewarding. On rare occasions these firms evolved into dynasties that lasted three or four generations. Familiar names like Ford, DuPont, Rothschild, Bombardier, and many more evolved across different borders and industries but began as family startups.

Family support and involvement is still a critically important element in generating small business startups. However, the family platform for starting and building a business is under siege in the face of globalization and the unprecedented rate of change that comes with globalism and the technology revolution. Conventional goals, like building a family empire and consolidating wealth for generations to come, are finding new avenues by creating abundant wealth more quickly while reducing the role of the family platform back to a source of startups. The family unit provides a unique ecosystem for encouragement and support, which may still be the single most important mechanism to promote startups, but the life expectancy of the businesses created is much shorter. In fact, we can expect reduced longevity for most companies in a world dominated by change.

Family Entrepreneur is a story about four individuals entrenched in different family businesses, each with unique challenges that can only result from merging family and business within the context of the modern global market. These four are determined to solve their individual issues by taking a new course offered by Sam Macleod, who has mentored all of them previously. Sam leads them through analysis of the pitfalls of being in family business using anecdotes and observations from his life-long career as a serial entrepreneur. The sessions are seen through the eyes of Mary O'Brien, who has been plagued with doubt about continuing in the family business or striking out on her own. As Mary engages in the sessions and the discussions with the other participants, her decision becomes clear. Anyone involved in a family business or interested in becoming an entrepreneur will relate to the issues and solutions that evolve out of these discussions.

CHAPTER ONE

Duty: A Path of Good Intentions

November 3, 2013

There was too much time for me to think. It was only a fifty kilometre drive out of the city, but it was taking an eternity. This excursion was an exercise in futility and a waste of vacation time. I was doubtful about finding a solution to my problem. Rain pelted the windows as I drove along the muddied country road. The weather mirrored my mood. Five years acting as office manager and jack-of-all-trades in my brother Ted's growing plumbing business. Three years since our younger brother, Tommy, had joined the company. A year since Tommy was given shares without regard to my contribution. Regardless, I thrived on the chaos of a growing family business. It was up to me to tie down the loose ends, build relationships with key suppliers, mend the problems with frustrated clients, smooth over any issues in the office, deal with our bank, collect accounts, convince suppliers to extend longer terms on our bigger jobs, and whatever else was required on a daily basis. My brothers were in the field doing "the work." Yet there seemed to be no way I would be getting shares. As a woman filling the mundane role of running the office, I was replaceable. Only two months before Ted had sat me down for a serious one-on-one about the future. For one brief moment I thought he might offer me equity, instead he confirmed what I already knew. In his eyes it was still a man's world.

"Mary, you really should think about getting married and having a family. I know you love your nieces and nephews but time's passing you by. We can work it out here if you're off for a while, and you'll always have a job here if you want it."

I could have shoved one of his precious plungers down his throat. Guaranteeing me a job! I should've quit on the spot. Only one problem — this was about family. As I drove down the muddy road, tears were welling up. How could you walk out on family? There was such a pervading sense of duty. Family loyalty was ingrained in my psyche for as long as I could remember. My father never questioned the need if one of his four siblings asked for help. Self-sacrifice was expected. But shouldn't it work both ways? I loved our business. Why couldn't my brothers see it?

In the meantime I had been improving myself in order to meet the needs of *their* business. I was constantly taking courses. The tech revolution was a potential boon for all small ventures, but it magnified the challenge of staying current. So many opportunities were clear to me. We could expand our reach, increase our controls, move our trucks around more efficiently, and market ourselves effectively on a small budget. These courses paid off. Our systems were right up to date. We had a presence on social media. Our customer follow-up was excellent. Feedback influenced decisions on equipment purchases and staffing, but I had to be subtle. My classes were supplemented by adding staff with additional expertise and I hired well. The creativity of the office team was reflected in our web page and in the online promotions we had been using, but the main upside was growth, both top line and bottom line. My brothers paid lip service to all of this. To their credit, the team in the field was a happy, cohesive unit that did high quality work. We had become the plumber of choice for several major home builders in the area. Ted had great relationships with the on-site staff for all of them. That was his strength.

As for me, other opportunities were emerging, if I wanted them. My LinkedIn network was growing. There had already been job offers. Two years earlier I had taken my first webinar offered by Online Studies Inc., a program called "Everyday Entrepreneur." My logic had been that if I couldn't convince my brothers to recognize my contribution, maybe it was time to try going out on my own. That course was an eye opener. The instructor was Sam Macleod, a crusty older guy with a big heart. He made me realize why I loved the business. He made me appreciate and trust my instincts, but the course itself whetted my appetite to lead. The section on team building made me realize that my brothers and I were operating two quite distinct businesses within one framework with two very different teams. It worked because of trust, explicit on my part and assumed on theirs. As long as I accepted things as they were it might continue to work. But after that webcast program, I considered myself an entrepreneur, a disruptor, one who challenges the status quo. For the last two years I'd played emotional ping pong between duty and desire. It had been hell.

This past summer I'd received an update from Online Studies. Sam was introducing a new webinar called "Family Entrepreneur." It was going to be the next step in his plan for a whole series on various forms of entrepreneurship. I was invited to apply for the prototype group to help define the program prior to initiating the webcasts. Directions were to include a summary of my experience and any personal challenges encountered within a family business. While I was nearly saturated with the "family" aspect of business, I decided to submit an application. Three weeks later I was accepted, provided I was available for the first two weeks of November. The boys gave me the time off on the premise that I would work offsite, but the time counted for one week of my ten weeks of accumulated vacation — generous to a fault.

I was looking forward to a live seminar and the opportunity to meet Sam, but I was doubtful it would help me much with my brothers. Four participants had been chosen. We would be the guinea pigs as Sam refined his new program. All of us had taken one of his webinars but none of us had met him or each other. I knew nothing about the other three. No names had been shared so I couldn't even Google them.

I was headed for the Speyside Mill, a well-known country inn and spa, and as I got closer, the thought of the seminar dragged me out of my misery. I pulled into the parking lot just after the rain stopped, and I could see very few cars. I parked and wheeled my lone suitcase into the reception area. I was immediately greeted by Mike Reynolds, who I recognized from the webinar. During the course Mike had been one of the three live participants we could see online, but only at the end had Sam revealed that Mike was a planted foil. Mike had acted out the role of the naïve rookie who thought entrepreneurship came easy and that the rewards were huge. It felt like I knew him, certainly people like him, maybe even worked with a couple. So meeting him first put me at ease.

"You're Mike Reynolds, aren't you? I recognize you from the Everyday Entrepreneur sessions."

This drew an instant laugh.

"Everyone remembers Mike the bumbler who just doesn't get it. I played that part to perfection in my first live session with Sam long before the webinar was even contemplated. Tim Davidson, the founder of Online Studies, was there too. I guess they decided no one else could fill my role quite as well. So you're either Mary O'Brien or Donna Simmonds. I'm guessing Mary."

"Good guess. What gave me away?"

"Just a hunch," he said with a quirky smile on his face. "So, before you check in let me give you a quick outline of the program. It should be familiar to you. Sam is pretty rigid in his approach. You'll have the morning and early afternoon to yourself. There's Wi-Fi here so all of you can work as you need. Our sessions run for two hours, from three to five, then there's a social hour/coffee klatch for the group to get to know each other and do some brainstorming. Your evenings are free. It's a proven formula similar to the way he structures the webinars, only, as you know, there the social part comes through an online chat."

I remembered the follow up chats fondly. I had learned almost as much from them as I did from the webinar and had picked up a number of LinkedIn connections for my network.

"You're the first one here, but I expect everyone else shortly. The first coffee hour is at five, which will give you a chance to meet the others."

I checked in and moved into my room in one of the out-buildings — once a storage room for the old stone millworks — with the river running right below my window. The room, which showcased the original thick stone walls, was furnished entirely with antiques, and was topped off with a gas-burning fireplace, which was a great addition for a cold damp afternoon. The next two hours flew by, and before I knew it I was back in the lounge, sipping my coffee of choice, a decaf latte, just as the next member of the group arrived. As I prepared to greet her, I decided to keep my family issues to myself for the moment. My intention was to seek Sam out and discuss those matters privately. Otherwise the course itself should give me some ideas. But there was no sign of Sam that night.

Donna Simmonds was not at all what I'd expected. Since Mike had mentioned her name, I'd found three possible candidates online. This one was in her early fifties, which meant that Mike recognizing me was no particular compliment, although she was quite elegant. She was well dressed in designer jeans, an azure-blue cashmere sweater, no coat, and knee-high soft and supple black leather boots. I had a similar pair. Still, she was twenty plus years older than me. My first reaction was that she was quite preoccupied and somewhat stressed, even frazzled. That perception would change very little over the next two weeks that we spent at the inn. Despite her state of mind she was very friendly and was soon sipping her own decaf latte as we got to know each other. On the surface she seemed to be what I aspired to become. As we settled into conversation, she described her experience with Online Studies.

"I was in their very first web series with Sam. My business was just about to take off, or at least it did once I followed some of his advice. The team-building part was the key. Once I added some much-needed talent our sales took off. My business is online retailing. I'm a designer. Perhaps you've heard of No Labels? We keep getting confused with that political group but our reputation is growing."

I had heard of them and I'd just read more during my quick and dirty research. I'd actually dismissed her as a possibility based on her success. My first reaction was: how did a girl from a little plumbing business get in a group with a fashion genius, frazzled or not? I didn't have long to consider the reason because the next member of our group arrived before I could make a comment. Steve Jacobi was about my age, perhaps a few years older. In contrast to Donna he seemed laid back. Having arrived late, he appeared remarkably calm, apparently travelling on a motorcycle because he was carrying his helmet under one arm while being totally clad in leather from head to toe, still gleaming from the most recent bout of rain. He was much less intimidating than Donna. It was a plus for my damaged ego that I hadn't heard of his business, which was an import-export firm dealing primarily in India. The main product was granite and marble stones used in the housing industry. The company imported the stones then distributed to fabricators across the country, but they also created various products themselves, primarily countertops for kitchens and bathrooms. Apparently the distribution was the core of the business. The original business, which was fabrication, had become secondary. He was interesting but very unassuming when I asked about his background.

"My father started the business. He emigrated from Italy as a boy right after the war. When he was about twenty he went back to visit family and came away with a love of stone, especially marble and granite. He returned to Italy for two years to apprentice and became an expert. That's how our stone fabricating business began. All our stones came from Italy for the first thirty years. Most people don't realize that India is a prime source of raw granite. The Italians were there first, buying rough stones and sending them back to Italy to be polished. That was our original source, but with global competition we had to go directly to India. We built some strong contacts early on, which lead us into distribution. My dad preferred making product. He'd roll over in his grave if he knew what we've done, but there are more light colours of granite available in India and they're in demand. More importantly, the Indians have finally perfected the polishing process. Distribution gives us buying power. My brother-in-law or I go there once or twice year. Mainly I go. It's unbelievable how much things have changed since I first went ten years ago."

I worked with a number of other fabricators who used granite so we had something to talk about. The builders selected the maker, but I had to coordinate the installation with our plumbing staff so I had learned a fair amount about the product. When we were doing renovations we would sometimes recommend suppliers for the counters and they would often return the favour. I had several in my network. For a few minutes Donna was left out of the conversation while we discussed some of the trends in the housing accessory trade. She did come alive when Steve started talking about the pros and cons of working in India. Donna was importing garments and had been there several times, which both excited and unnerved me. Did I belong with this group?

Then a new arrival changed the topic once again, but it wasn't the fourth member of the group. He didn't show up that night. Mike had brought over Tim Davidson, the owner of Online Studies, to meet us. All of us had expected Sam. When Donna asked about him, Tim tried to explain his absence.

"Sam's an enigma. He has a genuine passion for

entrepreneurship that he articulates like no one else, but fundamentally he's a loner. Still, people gravitate to him even when he hides, like tonight. He'll be at his best tomorrow, but he won't come for coffee after and he won't join us for dinner. That's just Sam."

The evening wound down quickly. We had the inn to ourselves, one of the benefits of mud season, so Tim had arranged for a small buffet. We were offered several salads and either poached salmon or grilled chicken. I chose a little of each. The conversation fizzled since all of us were tired, leading the conclave to break up early. By nine o'clock I was in bed immersed in the struggles of *Downton Abbey*, where the problems were much more overwhelming than mine.

CHAPTER TWO

Sam and the Routine

Our fourth didn't arrive until showtime the next afternoon. The rest of us spent the day in our rooms cramming a full day's work into a few hours. All of us had the 24/7 work ethic, so being offsite hardly slowed us down. That would be the pattern for the next two weeks.

Three o'clock came fast enough. The setup was a little unusual — not as intimate as the webinars, which almost gave you the feeling of being one-on-one with Sam, even though you knew there were others online as well as three in the workshop. For starters there were four of us in the program, plus Tim and Mike, who were video recording in the back of the room, invading our privacy. I wondered how that distraction would work or if it would limit the dialogue. Free and open conversation was a critical element of Sam's style. Apparently he had struggled with this when he started with the web-based seminars. Mike told me that Sam had rigidly adhered to a maximum of three people in his live sessions. It had taken Tim quite a while to convince him to address a larger audience. That's why there were always three in the studio workshop no matter how many were watching online. While Sam had perfected looking into the camera and reaching his audience effectively, he never participated in the live chats after the sessions.

We all felt that we knew him, but how could we? You could feel the tension in the room building as we contemplated his arrival.

With two minutes to go, Jeff Michaels, the fourth member of the group, walked in, introduced himself, and sat down, offering no background information and no explanation. He was in his mid-twenties at best. His shaved head was a distraction, but something about him seemed familiar. I had no time to consider why. Precisely at three o'clock Sam walked in. He went around the room quickly, shaking everyone's hand, addressing each of us by name, and then settled into his position at the front of the room. He was agile enough despite greying hair streaked with natural blond highlights. He was dressed in jeans and a vintage U of T sweatshirt that looked like it had survived since his undergraduate years along with comparable tennis shoes and no socks. His presence made the room come alive. Tim and Mike were so deferential that they slipped into the background for the next two hours. We just forgot that they were there.

As was his way, Sam jumped right in. "So. 'Family Entrepreneurship.' Is that an oxymoron?" The direct challenge was familiar but not exactly what we expected. "Seriously, can a family-based entity embrace all the attributes we've agreed upon for entrepreneurs? Can you build effective teams? Can you have fair compensation? Who leads? Where do the needs of the business rank? How about accountability? Isn't it really a commune where the spoils are shared based on entitlement, not merit? There are tons of questions for us to consider, but let's settle on one thing first. Do you remember what I told you about a tax loss?"

I certainly did, but before I could answer Steve Jacobi jumped in.

"Yes, Sam. The word 'tax' is just an adjective, but the loss is still a loss."

Sam smiled for the first time. All of us hesitated. Sam had come in with a bang, which none of us had expected. "That's right. So let's agree up front that in our context the word 'family' is also an adjective — one with a ton of implications, most of which we will consider, but we're going to focus on the premise that an entrepreneur is still an entrepreneur. Our goal is to make the family ecosystem an effective environment for entrepreneurship, regardless of all the pitfalls, and there are many."

At that point he paused for a sip from his water bottle and I started to breathe again, but then off he went.

"How does each of you fit into a family business scenario? Share just the bare bones for the rest of us to know. How about you, Mary?"

"I've spent five years in my brother's business, and now there are two brothers and myself. My role is administration."

"You're next, Donna."

Donna was still a little frazzled and almost barked her response like a military recruit. "I have been the CEO of my company for seven years. My two daughters have been heavily involved for the past three years."

Sam took another sip from the bottle, which was almost empty. Maybe he was as geared up as the rest of us. "How about you, Jeff. What's your story?"

Jeff was laid back and not even slightly intimidated by Sam. "Just considering it. My dad wants me to join his business. I'm pretty happy doing what I'm doing now."

Sam turned toward Steve, but he didn't have to wait for an answer. "It's been twelve years for me, starting with my dad, but now there's just me and my brother-in-law."

I still couldn't get over the pace. Sam had never been like this in the online sessions; he was more laid-back. Was this a new Sam, or was it his way to grab our attention? As I looked around the room, I read a similar reaction on the faces of my new associates. Sam seemed to realize this, because from that point he settled into a more normal pattern. As he did, we all began to relax, hoping he would revert to telling anecdotes about his own career.

"The family business is like motherhood. It's an institution, one of the cornerstones of the American dream. It requires an entrepreneurial spirit, but is it really entrepreneurship? It's an interesting debate, a little like the nature-nurture dispute, whether entrepreneurs are born or made. You know that I believe entrepreneurship is routed on the foundation of opportunity. Recognizing viable opportunities and acting on them are key factors in launching a career as an entrepreneur. Many family businesses are initially tied much closer to necessity, meaning the opportunity is often more limited. But that does change as the business becomes established. Initially success is tied to sweat equity more than innovation. The goals are modest and more immediate. Duty and obligation play huge roles. Independence and upward mobility for the family unit are major motivations. But then again all of these are factors with most entrepreneurs. The stakes are high. Failure simply isn't an option. Determination is the major factor in success. That's certainly true for all entrepreneurs. What do you think?"

Steve Jacobi was eager to make the first comment. "From my experience the family business did provide the initial opportunity. Not only that, seeing what my dad was doing and helping as a kid I think I experienced both the nature and the nurture sides of what it takes to be an entrepreneur. You learn a lot from example. I was definitely groomed to take over. Not forced, but the assumption that I would join the business was always there. My uncle finally left and started on his own over that very issue because he knew that the line of succession passed through me. He would never get the opportunity to lead. Our group discussed this quite a bit on the chats while I was taking your seminar online. There were quite a few people who were in some type of family business."

Sam was nodding in agreement. "There's a lot of evidence to support your point. In fact, entrepreneurship often peaks in the family business in the second generation, especially in very conventional family startups evolving from the need to make a living. The founders may be satisfied to achieve stability. The drivers come in the next generation, and that can create conflict. What's best for the business may not be what's best for the family and the foundation that the first generation built. The founders usually grow up in a culture of need and have a distinct memory of deprivation. If they have reasonable success, their children have no such experience, often growing up in a culture of gratification. The differences can be difficult to reconcile."

Donna was on the edge of her chair but didn't get a chance to comment because Jeff Michaels beat her to it. "What if the second generation isn't interested? Maybe they just don't like the business world. Or maybe they want to do their own thing; something completely different."

I wondered if Jeff was facing these issues himself. He looked pretty young and his appearance was screaming independence. Sam had us all engaged now as he continued.

"That can be a tough issue. Growing up in an environment of need leads to drive and determination. If the first generation is very successful then things come much easier to their children, whose interest in the business could be minimal. That's a much different scenario than for a lifestyle startup with less dynamic achievements where there are more obvious needs still to be met and different goals to accomplish. Both are entrepreneurial, life-changing achievements, but in a different stage of personal evolution. These are real dilemmas with a variety of solutions and distinct implications for the future of the business. You've all experienced my sessions so you know that I believe everyone has some level of entrepreneurial ability, but even those who are far to the right on the curve can have children with completely opposite tendencies. Perversely, one of the barriers to applying your entrepreneurial skills can be the success of your parents. Complacency can nullify leadership and ambition even though example can magnify both. Frankly, if the children do have similar abilities they probably will want to do their own thing either within or outside the family operation. They will naturally be inclined toward disruption. There's a whole series of possibilities regarding how generations will react. Over the next few days we'll get into specific aspects of these potential conflicts."

Sam was referring to his vaunted curve plotting out a normal distribution of entrepreneurial traits/abilities on the x-axis against the percentage of the population that demonstrated them on the y-axis. On the extreme left were those who had virtually no entrepreneurial interest or ability while on the extreme right were the entrepreneurial superstars that the public reveres as true entrepreneurs. All of us had a spot on that curve, and the more you understood the personal and business requirements to succeed as an entrepreneur, the better you could position yourself on the curve relative to others. Individual initiative could shift your position and your prospects. That's exactly what I was doing by building knowledge and understanding. The concept was the foundation of the Everyday Entrepreneur seminar series. Understand the phenomenon *and* understand yourself. Become more entrepreneurial in your thinking to manage your career, whether within your own business or not.

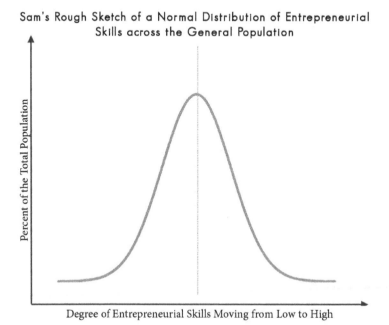

Sam's Rough Sketch of a Normal Distribution of Entrepreneurial Skills across the General Population

Percent of the Total Population

Degree of Entrepreneurial Skills Moving from Low to High

Mike was a good example. His role-playing in the webcasts was based on his initial attitude when he came to Sam as an aspiring entrepreneur. He had been looking for a quick and easy fix. His interest was all about the money and an easy life. By the time he finished the sessions with Sam, he had a strong sense of what was required and a new belief in what he might accomplish. Most people never make the connection. He and I had discussed this the day before. His self-confidence and work ethic belied the fact that he had been a lost, misguided soul with poor prospects a few years ago. I looked back to see him and noticed that he was as immersed in Sam's discussion as anyone else, camera in hand. Then I remembered Mike's father had been a successful entrepreneur but had died fairly young, leaving a confused teenaged Mike to work things out on his own. This conversation was close to home.

Then Sam switched gears, moving into his first anecdote.

"Most people seem to feel that duty and guilt either draw them into a family business against their better judgement or keep them there when they want to move on."

I could feel a lump in my throat. Duty was a heavy burden, one that had kept me put for the past two years. I wondered where Sam was going with this.

"I don't agree. Those issues are more about getting out, not getting in. Every entrepreneur has to have an end game, whether they're in a family entity or not. Never forget that. Nothing lasts forever, especially these days. The one constant is change. As for me, I'm an accidental entrepreneur, and if it weren't for a sense of duty I might have missed the opportunity to be one. On March 29, 1969, my world changed dramatically. At the time, I was in the midst of year-end exams during my master's year. I had just taken the first set of interviews for a position to teach economics at the local college. There was no plan for me to go into business. That morning my father-in-law suffered a fatal coronary thrombosis. Five weeks later I was sitting at his desk working beside his son, engaged in a one-year commitment to help my friend adjust to running the small family business. That one-year agreement turned into a lifelong career as an entrepreneur, a calling for which I was meant but could easily have missed had it not been for a sense of duty. The family connection provided the opportunity. It wasn't entirely an accident. I agonized over the decision, compelled to go ahead regardless, but I was intrigued by the prospects. Against all advice I elected to fulfil my obligation and take the chance of combining family with career. The prevailing sentiment was get in if you must, but get out as fast as you can.

"I recognized many possibilities and once I made a decision I relished the idea that I could influence the outcome. The culture of control and playing politics inherent in large corporations weren't nearly as appealing. We have to recognize the opportunities that we get, not just those that we want. Sitting back and waiting for the right one is too passive. All opportunities are not created equal. Every idea isn't an opportunity, and every opportunity isn't viable. A family business can be a burden, but it also gives you something that many never get: a platform to launch a career as an entrepreneur. In particular, women may find better opportunities within their family business and that's significant in an era where the glass ceiling still exists."

Even I had to admit that the business had given me opportunities that I wouldn't have had otherwise, but my experience didn't fully support that last statement. My future was limited by more of a concrete ceiling, one that was far from hidden. Still, whether officially an owner or not, I considered myself to be an integral part of that business, which was the real dilemma. I knew I wasn't a tier-two participant in the family or in the business. I didn't feel entitled to anything but an opportunity based on performance.

Sam continued. "Of course, most large corporations were once startups or were assembled by acquiring smaller companies, but a surprising number of large private and public companies either started as family operations or still have large shareholdings in the founding family's hands. When does the family entrepreneur become the family manager? When does the family startup become the family enterprise? Does entrepreneurship survive longer in the family firm? There has to be an entry level for new businesses and the family version is still the most common. Can you name some of the better known behemoths that started this way? Don't be shy, just shout them out."

"Ford, Wal-Mart, and Bombardier," I shouted.

"Levi-Straus, Thomson Reuters, and Weston's," said Donna.

Steve called out "Power Corp, Cargill, and Trump."

Jeff didn't offer anything. That bothered Sam.

"C'mon Jeff, only North American companies were mentioned. We live in a global economy. How about names like Toyota, Samsung, Fiat, and Tata? There are a lot more out there. If you look at the pattern of how these major players evolved, it seems that the critical generation is actually the third or fourth. If the family can sustain its entrepreneurial character effectively through several generations the company can become nationally or internationally significant, maybe even faster in today's environment. The acid test seems to be that third generation, where the principals are most likely to become complacent or incompetent. This is the stage that most successful family companies are either sold or decline and fail. A rare few make it through the gauntlet to become independent major players. Roughly 2 percent of family businesses make it to the fourth generation. I'm surprised the percentage is even that high, and I have little doubt that it will decline farther in the current environment. If they do survive, the firms that maintain strong family leadership often outperform their publically owned competitors. Can you suggest some reasons why?"

Steve seemed to be well read on the subject.

"I'm sure it has to do with purpose and vision. I read somewhere that the established family business doesn't need some philosophical mission statement for direction and motivation. Those businesses have a real *cause* to preserve, increase the family wealth and influence, which is deeply ingrained in the younger generations if they have the ability and interest to continue the family's aspirations. That makes sense to me."

"I read something similar," said Donna. "It's actually one of the things that influenced me to bring my two daughters into my business. The younger generation often sees themselves as stewards of a legacy. But they don't have an exit strategy, which you recommended for all of us. Instead they are focused on handing the ship over in better shape than they received it."

I didn't have anything to offer. I was frozen on the peripheral of a family business in its early stage with no insight into the future, at least for now.

Jeff finally added a comment.

"I agree that there's often a sense of duty to protect the family's interest, but don't forget these individuals have been raised in a culture of success. For some it's a compulsion that more or less parallels your bell curve, Sam. A small percentage of family start-ups will last that long by sustaining an entrepreneurial culture from generation to generation that gives them an advantage. Leadership is in their blood. If they have the ability, the odds are in their favour to continue or as an alternative to start their own venture. Either way, networks already exist. Funding is never an issue since the banks are soliciting them based on substantial family assets. Long-term success must go back to the founder. These companies were built by strong individuals for whom the end game was to build a family-controlled empire that they percolated by teaching and sustaining an entrepreneurial philosophy. It can become predestination."

Sam smiled. "Welcome to the class, Jeff. I was wondering when you were going to show up."

I wanted to add something, not just sit there as a bystander. I had been listening and considering what the others had said.

"Maybe the owners of these companies have better foresight, Sam. You always emphasize our fast-paced economy. Public companies are all about performance and short-term results to satisfy shareholders, but the stability the founders of private companies were searching for can give their descendants a different opportunity. If you're the CEO of a company controlled by your family and have their support, you can make better decisions by considering a longer-term perspective without worrying about being ousted. It's like politics. How many bad decisions are made to get re-elected?"

Sam was smiling.

"Not a bad analogy Mary. We should all be concerned that the pressure to perform in both government and large corporations can compromise decisions at all levels. That trend in combination with policies like 'too big to fail' has put us in an economic quagmire for the last five years. It's going to be much more difficult for companies to survive for generations in the current environment.

"It looks like we have the makings of a solid group here. So if no one objects I'll cut it off there for today, but I have one last thing to discuss. As you know you've been invited here to help us lay out this new course, one we've been asked for repeatedly. You were selected based on feedback from your online sessions as well as the nature of your family businesses, your roles, and your particular issues. We didn't announce this beforehand because we wanted participants who were committed, but Tim is covering all your costs. You are officially part of the creative team so I'm counting on you to keep the pressure on and the ideas flowing. There is one more thing I'd like you to do while you're here. I've just been given a contract by Binkley-Miller Publishers to write a book based on the Everyday Entrepreneur sessions. I'm pretty excited. It'll allow me to reach a much broader audience."

Everyone in the room applauded. All of us had an appreciation for Sam, who had influenced every one of us.

"That's right, my greatest entrepreneurial challenge yet is going to be creating Sam the author. Anyway, I want to introduce some new concepts in the book, so I'd like to bounce a quote off you at the end of each session for you to consider. That includes Tim and Mike as well. Is that all right?"

We were all pleased for Sam and ready to help him out. The idea of contributing anything to a book was exciting for me. I was sure that he'd have some interesting new ideas.

"So the first concept is based on the fast-moving global economy Mary just mentioned, which has played havoc with job stability and made it difficult for young people to launch their careers and for seniors to hold on to theirs. It's a premise that all of you should bear in mind as you assess your future. Basically, the quote goes 'The most important skill you can learn today is the ability to create and manage your own career.' It's something that I feel is absolutely critical. Think about it. Enjoy your coffee klatch."

CHAPTER THREE

Coffee and Conversation

The four of us plus Mike regrouped in the lounge. It wasn't mandatory but all of us knew that follow-up discussion was key to what we would get out of the sessions. Mike said that the inn was short-staffed since they were usually closed for the first two weeks of November — a pre-Christmas rush break during mud season — so we literally had the inn to ourselves. Mike ran the espresso machine and made the coffee. The first point of business wasn't what you might think. The coffee klatch name had to go — there was unanimous agreement on that. After about twenty minutes of the most vigorous debate of the day it came down to a choice between "The *Brew*haha" and "The Coffee Grinder." In the end, the heated nature of the debate won the day, and even though it was a different kind of brew, the name Brewhaha stuck.

Once we got past that levity we started to discuss the session. No one, including me, seemed interested in revealing any family issues. Sam's bearing was the first thing all of us had noticed. As usual Steve took the lead. "Sam was far more intense than I remember. It was definitely the advanced course compared to my first go around with him. He seems to expect more from us."

Donna joined in. "I'm not sure it has much to do with us. He has to be wound up about the book and frankly he *should* expect more from us. We've been through his main subject matter. I follow his program of giving back religiously by providing a funding subsidy to the two students with the best startup proposals submitted out of the fashion program at George Brown every spring. The ideas get better every year and the pitches are far more comprehensive than they were just three years ago. He's preaching to the converted. We're here because we are on the right side of the curve. Sam wants us to take it to the next level."

It was my turn to offer an opinion. "The book is great news. I think his message will go over really well. I wonder how he'll go about writing it. His sessions are fairly unique, but I don't know how's he going to convey the same message in the book. As far as today goes, I liked the more active exchange where we're all more involved, but when we get into more detail he'll probably revert to controlling the dialogue, don't you think?"

Jeff stayed non-committal, quietly sipping his espresso. I noticed he had dumped in three heaping spoonfulls of sugar so it was really more like syrup. Cheryl and I stuck to our decaf lattes while Steve had a cappuccino and Mike had a regular black coffee.

Mike was more forthcoming. "I don't think so. All of you have something to offer from experience. I'm a little surprised at my own reaction today. You didn't get in to too many issues, but the whole family thing hit home for me. Sam really had me think-ing about my dad and what might have been. I'm a little envious of all of you being in a family business. I never had the chance."

Steve spoke up with real feeling. "Don't be. It's a mixed blessing.

His edge caught Jeff's attention. "Tell us more. My dad's pres-suring me and the whole family. I don't want to do it."

Steve withdrew as fast as he'd jumped in. "Not right now. I'm going up to my room. I have some calls to make. Sorry."

He clearly didn't want to open up yet and he seemed to have some issues with his brother-in-law. Jeff decided to leave as well, which wasn't surprising based on his limited interaction up to that point. That left me, Donna, and Mike, which, as it turned out, became the norm, at least when we stayed in.

As soon as they left Donna weighed in. "What did you think of that? Steve seemed so laid back last night. He definitely has some family issues to resolve,"

Mike looked her right in the eye, intending to nip gossip before any started. "Donna, you all do. That's one of the reasons we invited you and probably the main reason all of you came."

I decided to change the subject. Like Steve, I wasn't ready to talk about my issues. Not yet.

"What did you make of Sam's quote at the end?"

Donna was happy to offer her opinion. "I think Sam hit on a huge problem: managing your career is critical at any age. Young kids are breaking down my door willing to do anything to get started in a career related to fashion. At the same time, I have several experienced friends who have lost their jobs and have been shifting from one contract position to another. They're used to stability. None of them expected to be looking for work in their fifties. I don't agree, but their experience is almost considered irrelevant because today's job skills are so new and different. I'm not sure any generation has had to deal with this type of new reality. So hard to get started and being forced out early. My business needed help, which was one of the reasons I brought my two daughters into it. I had a need, but like so many young people so did they. Not everyone is as lucky as I was to have people there to help out. Then there's this whole trend for so-called Mompreneurs trying to find careers that they can balance with their family needs. Those kinds of jobs have to be invented, designed to fill a specific employment need. Thank God for technology. Between the networking possibilities on social media and the low-cost marketing almost anyone can do online, there are so many more possibilities to create your own job."

That was a good summary. I had experienced the same thing.

"You're right, we have a steady stream of young people coming in every day, most of them overqualified and often educated in completely different fields, willing to do anything. And of course older people as well. We've hired two because they're very stable. It's hard to believe that the young people will stay for long if the economy improves, but we've started to see an increase in something else. We have more young people applying right out of high school. They don't feel that it's worth going to college, so they look for apprenticeships. They see plumbing as China-proof."

Mike seemed interested in our observations.

"There's another dimension to Sam's concern. If you think back it comes up in every session of his basic series. Sam has a lot of concerns about the combination of big business, big government, and globalization and their impact on individualism. We have comparative advantages and disadvantages in North America, but some of the latter translate into structural unemployment. Big businesses will not solve that issue. We all know that they will invest for profit wherever that can be maximized. As you pointed out, Mary, that's short-term thinking based on today's results. It's going to take small business with a local bias to start dealing with these pockets of unemployment. Detroit is a good example. Sam taught us all that every problem is an opportunity. Entrepreneurs are well aware that real estate and labour are cheap in Detroit and are taking advantage of that opportunity. It's not a quick fix but it will move the needle. Sam is adamant that we have to teach the young to create their own jobs or they will be mired in a shrinking middle class with limited upward mobility — the antithesis of the American dream. He feels that entrepreneurship of necessity, especially family businesses at many levels, is on the rise and more important than ever. It's one of the reasons he is developing this new web cast. Tim thinks he convinced him for the sake of expanding Online Studies but Sam is doing it because he believes in the need."

By that time it was 6:30. Mike had ordered pizzas, which arrived right on time, perfect for a group of workaholics. Mike brought some up to the others while Donna and I ate together and continued our conversation. Before long it was time to head to our rooms. There was a lot to digest besides the pizza.

CHAPTER FOUR

Is Leadership Effective?

It was only the second day, but it was a familiar drill so the routine was easily established. Each of us was preoccupied with our day-to-day responsibilities in the morning. I called my brother Ted and he was elated that I was available from 7:00 a.m. until 3:00 p.m. every day. Even better, if something critical came up I could work on it overnight. There wasn't one question about what I was doing or how it was going.

When we met up at three Sam seemed refreshed. I wasn't sure how he spent his time away from us. Maybe he was writing the book. Whatever he did there was no sign of him around the inn. I found out later that he lived nearby. Regardless, he greeted us all warmly and easily shifted back into his program.

"There are so many combinations of relationships that convert a company into a family business. Some analysts feel this only happens if there's a second generation, but believe me, it often develops early in the startup phase. I personally have worked in different businesses with my mother, my mother-in-law, my brother, my brother-in-law, my wife, my sister-in-law, my daughters, my son, several nephews, and my grandson. I'm still speaking to all of those who are still alive, and those that aren't at least died naturally. One or two of these working relationships were just seasonal student jobs, but most of them were the real thing, including many bumps in the road, all of them deeper because they involved family. There's a different dynamic with family participation that is reflected in increased sensitivity, heightened by a sense of entitlement from being part of the ownership group. Like it or not, many issues become personal. In the early stages, compromise happens more frequently and to a greater degree; later on, not so much. Leadership is often blurred and job descriptions may not exist. Sometimes strategy is hammered out around the dinner table. The line between home and work can be non-existent.

"The founder and leader becomes a fixer and can be dragged into personal issues on a regular basis. For many small businesses, where earning a living remains the sole purpose, this never changes. But I caution you, don't demean these lifestyle entrepreneurs. These founders are genuine entrepreneurs who routinely solve a host of problems, and much less would happen at that level in our economy without them. These businesses provide a critical gateway for aspiring entrepreneurs. If necessity is the mother of invention, opportunity is the father of entrepreneurship. Fear of failure is a huge motivation because the livelihood of the family depends on them. The whole operation sits squarely on the shoulders of that founder. This situation may sound like the good old days, but such dependence is still widespread and growing in importance as small business creation expands in the face of structural unemployment. Families still fund startups when they can, and especially when others won't.

"When I worked as a small business consultant one of my favourite clients was a company in which seven brothers worked in the construction industry. The founder had started as a construction labourer when he was sixteen. When he was eighteen his father co-signed a loan for him to buy a backhoe. Maybe that's where their sense of family obligation began."

There was a gasp beside me, which I think came from Jeff, but Sam didn't seem to notice.

"He was actually the second oldest brother. As the contracts got bigger he needed to hire and turned to the most convenient option — his brothers. Today that company does over $50 million in annual sales and all seven brothers are still there and remain the only shareholders. The work environment was very old school. Each brother started in the field as a labourer and learned the most basic elements of the business. They were a rough and tumble bunch. Every one of them went through a baptism under fire with no favours. The structure of the organization was tough to comprehend, *but it worked!* By the time I joined them two brothers were inside, one estimating and submitting tenders and one coordinating the crews. The other five each had their own crew in the field. Responsibilities were independent as there was complete trust among the brothers. Decisions were usually made by committee, although the older more senior brothers had more sway when necessary. Monthly meetings were chaotic, near mayhem, but they were always fun, ending with a drink and a laugh. The ability to laugh is invaluable in any business, but even more critical in a family one. I had insisted on these meetings, and initially they were volatile and unmanageable for me, but before long I was setting the agenda without resistance. The bedlam remained but the focus was tighter. By the end of each meeting I welcomed the drink.

"This is where I first saw the communal aspect of a family business work well to keep the business vibrant and avoid division. All seven brothers took the same compensation. As much as they would argue about decisions to buy equipment or how much each worker would get as a raise, I never saw them disagree about their own compensation. It stayed equal even when responsibility didn't. The principle of equal pay is common in some families, but I've never seen it on that scale before and for so long."

None of us had experienced anything like that. Fair compensation was a major issue in business of any kind. Steve had some doubts.

"Sam, do you think that's a sustainable model for any business? How much more successful could that business be with clear job definition, more discipline, and proper leadership?"

Now Sam was grinning from ear to ear. "That's just it, Steve. It's the dilemma I raised yesterday. Is the term family entrepreneur an oxymoron? Is it possible to be true to your family and to the enterprise? Can you be an effective entrepreneur while making the compromises expected from family? Most people will make concessions for family that they would never make to anyone else, which is both a strength and a weakness for any family business. In this case, the work ethic was strong and there was clear job definition, they simply agreed to rise or fall together as a team."

Jeff had a clear opinion. "What you've described couldn't happen twice. No one but a saint could live up to that kind of arrangement with so many players."

This comment made Sam laugh out loud. "Oh these boys were anything but saints. If I had to draw an analogy, their operation was more like being in the trenches together. If you made it through basic training and did battle you were one of the boys, no questions asked. It was a very chauvinistic operation, but that pretty much goes with the territory for construction. You would have loved the interview I went through to become their consultant. It made the inquisition look like a cakewalk. All seven sat around a boardroom table and grilled me for an hour. It was different, to say the least."

I winced at the mention of chauvinism, but I had seen these same attitudes between my brothers; tough exteriors, but loyal to a fault. All I wanted was for them to extend the same consideration to me. Regardless I felt obliged to defend the approach.

"I think I understand them, Sam. Didn't you say the company was profitable and grew dramatically? Who are we to define success for those brothers? If any company is flourishing, the owners determine how the profits are distributed. How did they remunerate people from outside the family? Besides, is success just about maximizing the growth and profitability of the business? That sounds like a public company to me, the ones we talked about yesterday, hung up on immediate results. Aren't you the one who preached balance in your first seminar series? It sounds to me that at the end of the day if these guys could sit down together, enjoy a drink and laugh, maybe they had it right and the rest of us may have it wrong. One key concept I've learned from you is that there are many types of entrepreneurs and many degrees of entrepreneurship. It seems to me that this group made things happen and found their own balance doing it. They may be unconventional, but it seems their approach works for them."

Dead silence for a minute. Maybe I had overstepped my bounds. I wasn't even the leader of a company, an aspiring junior partner at best. I didn't dare to look around the room. I had almost made a speech. But Sam enjoyed it.

"You're right. The results justify the means, but I still consider this family business and many others to be a form of socialized entrepreneurship with different rules and different standards. However, I also know that this can be an effective form of entrepreneurship that can mature into extremely successful companies. It also fosters a culture that produces future entrepreneurs, off-shoot businesses, and significant job creation. My story is rare and extreme, but it does highlight a whole range of areas that create leadership issues within a family business. Care to name a few for us to discuss?"

Steve named two. "Strategy and vision."

Jeff was equally quick. "Responsibility and accountability."

Donna was next. "Compensation and discipline."

I was thinking as fast as I could. "Decision-making and recruiting."

Sam offered no specific comment on any of our suggestions. "Those are all areas that must be dealt with in every business and for all entrepreneurs. They're demanding for individuals, frustrating in partnerships, and even more complicated within a family environment. Jeff is right; the formula I just described wouldn't work in most scenarios. Even two brothers can have a hard time operating within that structure. Usually there's a senior partner or founder who is the de facto leader and determines compensation. Most often this is the father or oldest brother, maybe mother or sister now, who starts a business like any other entrepreneur but for convenience or out of loyalty turns to the family for talent. Sometimes those hires are done on merit, but more often they are made for personal reasons rather than business savvy. In my first business we nurtured a family culture. We looked to the families of our employees when we were increasing our employment. Subject to having enough ability, these people brought loyalty to their jobs. Regardless, this policy was based on quick and convenient hiring, a practice most entrepreneurs follow. It's very common and can be all too expedient.

"Loyalty is a huge asset within the family and extended family of a small business. To some degree it can offset the lack of systems and controls because everyone cares about the success and image of the company. This culture of convenience works very well in smaller companies with fifty or less employees partially because the founder and leader knows every employee to some degree and partially because that same leader can oversee and handle most of the business issues relying upon the support network implicit in the family-owned operation. But this type of loyalty can become delusional and impair decision making. We'll talk more about that later.

"Convenient hires aren't limited to family scenarios. Founders of tech startups draw on university buddies for the same reasons: loyalty and availability. Depending on the ability, drive, and determination of the leader, this approach can even work in larger scenarios for a while, but as the company grows the need for systems, accountability, fair compensation, upward mobility, strategy, planning, and outside recruitment increases, requiring discipline. Every solo entrepreneur shares the same problems without the security blanket and support provided by the family network. But that support comes at a price, as it fosters obligation, which clouds solutions. Even the independent entrepreneur relies on the special loyalty that comes from working closely with a small work force."

Sam reached for the water bottle again. He had been talking more than before. Steve took the opportunity to ask a question.

"Sam, don't you think that vision, discipline, and organization are more critical than trust and loyalty for the success of any startup?"

"Was your father organized when he started? Did he have a clear vision of where his business could go? Was he disciplined about the right things? I doubt it. Opportunity is a moving target. Discipline grows out of determination and experience. Management techniques can be learned. Loyalty and trust can sustain small business owners through the learning curve. Leadership starts with people believing in you, followed by you justifying their trust and confidence by delivering results. A good leader hates to let his followers down. Loyalty sustains determination. That's one key to the early success of a family business. Maybe if we prepared people better for their startup phase many failures could be avoided, but for now loyalty builds leadership and vice versa."

Sam took another large mouthful of water. His bottle was empty.

"Our goal in setting the parameters of this new webcast was to help people understand the issues and challenges they will face as family entrepreneurs, both as business leaders and as family members. I think I want all interested parties to take the first program on entrepreneurship before this one. I just don't think we'll make much sense without them gaining some background on the business side first. These family factors are simply hurdles if they're understood, but they can easily become habits. Informalities can lead to a culture that can hamper the development and management of the business. If not addressed they can become insurmountable barriers to growth and improvement.

My sessions have never focused on how to deal with the issues. Rather, they focus on understanding them and pointing out that solutions exist. Solving the particular problem is the domain of the individual entrepreneur, subject to his or her circumstances. Every family is different and has to find appropriate solutions. I think the answers come easier if you have a grasp of entrepreneurship beforehand. Anyway, let's get back on topic and revisit the list of concerns you named earlier, starting with strategy and vision."

Those were the issues Steve had brought up, so he jumped in. "I'm relying on my own experience here. You were right Sam; my dad was really just earning a living. He loved what he did and he did it well, but he was preoccupied with day-to-day issues. He didn't really have a vision for the company beyond achieving independence and meeting his obligations, like sending me and my sister to college or giving my mother the house that she wanted. Providing for my uncle was part of the same thought process. The business was just a means to several ends, not an entity with potential. I don't think he fostered the opportunities that came along. You've told us often enough that the only thing we can count on is change. These jobs/businesses will come and go a lot faster in today's economy if they don't have a strategy and vision."

Donna was eager to comment. "C'mon, Steve. You're looking at a business started in 1950. Based on your age, your father probably married late. His priorities changed. People are better informed today. Support networks are everywhere. Advisors and mentors are in oversupply. How can we ever create enough wealth to keep all the financial planners in this country employed? I don't think you can start any business today without recognizing the need for a vision and a strategy to achieve it. I employ my daughters. My problem isn't having a vision or strategy it's convincing them to buy into it. The generation gap in family business is a bigger problem than a lack of direction."

There was some insight into Donna's problems. I wanted in on this discussion. I had seen both sides and put time and effort into studying how women were generating startups at a faster rate than men.

"I also think we have a gender difference here. More women are starting businesses. They're networking effectively and they're paying attention to mentors like Sam. A lot of these businesses will become family operations and they will have a vision, just like Donna has. I work with my two brothers. They're plumbers, both of whom have more in common with Steve's dad than they do with Donna. Right now they rely on me to think about these issues, whether they realize it or not. Believe me, there are still a lot of small businesses out there preoccupied with survival, not visualizing even a medium-term window."

At this point, Sam was actually on the edge of his chair. This was a more intense response than he expected.

"Good stuff, Donna and Mary. You're dead right about the gender issues. From work ethic to tech knowledge, the gender gap is narrowing, but I'm afraid I have to rein you in. The real point is that the family business itself is evolving and that some of the stereotypes are changing, just as they are for any small business. And Steve, don't undervalue lifestyle entrepreneurs like your dad. They still are initiating meaningful startups. So what's next? I think responsibility and accountability, wasn't it, Jeff?"

Jeff was ready. "There's many blind eyes turned in a family business. There can be a lot of ranting and raving, but little real accountability. You can fight, but can you fire? How do you fire your uncle or your brother or your daughter? There are tons of family hangers-on that are a drag on perfectly viable businesses."

"It can also go too far the other way," Steve added. "My father expected far more from me than any of his employees. If I messed up I couldn't hide it. He was always watching and he was all over me for mistakes. He wouldn't fire me but I was definitely accountable. There were enough times that I wanted to quit. He also made sure that his employees knew that I was being held to a higher standard. It was tough, but it made my transition to becoming the boss possible."

Sam was enjoying this. "Your father was a wise man, Steve. He picked the lesser of two evils, but lack of accountability or excessive accountability both cause problems. It's critical to find balance on this issue. Now, we need to pick up the pace a bit. Donna, I believe compensation and discipline were next."

She seemed a little distracted, preoccupied with the previous discussion. "Your dad was right on, Steve. I demand and expect more from my daughters than from any other employees. I don't see that changing. As far as compensation goes, Sam introduced the problem earlier. The seven brothers took equal rewards even when it wasn't warranted. Doesn't that lower performance to the level of the weakest link? Isn't it human nature to want fair compensation? How would that affect non-family employees who will recognize the difference in ability and performance? As far as discipline goes, family members think of themselves as owners even when they have junior roles. This can lead to a lot of abuse and little or no discipline. Even if they are held accountable, the consequences of mistakes are softened from what they should be, producing a sense of entitlement that compromises the culture and causes resentment."

No one else commented, which made Sam turn to me. "Decision-making and recruiting it is Mary."

It was late so I knew I wouldn't have to talk long. "Earlier you mentioned decisions by committee. I think that's ineffective and no way to make a good decision. I also think that the best decisions for the business often take a back seat to the best decisions for the family, which aren't one and the same. As far as recruiting goes, lack of it ties into Steve's earlier comment about strategy. It's tough to build your team. As the business grows the talent within the family won't fill the needs. Often there's duplication of both strengths and weaknesses. However, it's hard to attract ambitious employees when they see a company top-heavy with family executives or managers."

As I finished, Sam looked at his watch.

"Oh my, we're way past our time — it's 5:25. Tim, we're going to have to revise the subject for this session. On the other hand, the feedback and participation were great and that's hard to control. Let's wind this up now. No quote for tonight. Maybe that means two tomorrow. Have a good night."

CHAPTER FIVE

The Brewhaha Lives Up to the Name

Mike couldn't serve up the lattes and espresso fast enough. Steve was talking to Jeff in an angry tone.

"Don't do it. Stay out of the family business! I was an indentured labourer for the first six years. At that point my dad brought my brother-in-law Dave in and he didn't get the same treatment. Two years later my dad died. I'm just saturated with guilt about all the fights we had over the direction of the company during those last two years. I got my way but I'll never feel good about it because I never did convince him. Now I'm stuck with Dave and my sister always looking over my shoulder, asking if that's what dad would do. I'm ready to get out and do my own thing. You stick to your guns."

Jeff was a little shell-shocked. "Sorry man, I really didn't want to stir the pot. You need to wind down. I've got some wine upstairs if you're interested."

Steve was already turning for the door. "By the way, Donna, you didn't need to upstage me in there. The way you took my old man's side, I thought my sister was talking. I'm out of here."

A few minutes later we heard the sound of his motorcycle starting. It was already dark so I was alarmed how fast he took off. He was exactly like my brothers. If there was a disagreement at work, one of them always peeled out of there in his truck. Jeff stayed around for a while. I think he felt bad about upsetting Steve.

"It's not that my dad's a bad guy. Actually, he's the opposite, but I like running my own show, doing things the way I feel they should be done. I've built my own team, set my own goals, and made my own mistakes. I don't want the burden of supporting my family and I don't want them undermining my organization."

What organization was that? Donna looked over at me. She hadn't digested the last comment. Obviously she had dealt with the same issue from the opposite perspective. She hesitated but then spoke up.

"You're pretty cocky for someone who hasn't even walked in the door yet. Definitely don't let your dad pressure you, and take the time to think about all the pros and cons. But remember, Sam's adamant that opportunity is the foundation for entrepreneurship. I don't know your dad or anything about his business, but it could be the platform you need."

Jeff laughed. "That's just it. I don't need a platform. You've got to excuse me. I need some wine for myself."

So there we were, the same solid three as the night before. Mike had confided to me that he had had a drinking problem when he was younger but it was under control. He didn't show any signs of being tempted but I felt the need to keep him preoccupied and away from Jeff. That shaved head turned me off. Maybe I was stereotyping when I shouldn't.

"Well at least we're getting a sense of the issues that those two are here about," I said as Mike brought a second decaf latte for both Donna and I.

"Sorry girls, no chef tonight, but I've got the panini press heated up. Hope you like mozzarella, tomatoes, black olives, and ham on focaccia. Onions are an option."

That was appealing to me, onions and all, and looked even better when he produced a tomato salad with bocconcini cheese. Mike was proving to be a great short-order cook. Later he told us that he'd run a café up in cottage country. That's where he had met Sam and Tim. Mike was a good source of information regarding Sam. He was a serious disciple of the man. You could hear it in his voice when he talked about Sam's influence on his life.

"My mother actually saved the day. Sam had pretty well written me off when she went to see him. It turned out that he knew my dad. I didn't have a clue when I took his little summer session. I'd spent weeks in Homewood detoxing then had gone to the family cottage on Bass Island for the first time in three years, basically since my dad had died. I signed up with Sam for a lark. I have a significant trust fund. I thought I could use part of it to make some big bucks. It couldn't be that difficult. I was a jerk at first and Sam was hard on me for it. What you see in the webcast is pretty much the way he feels about the quick-fix mentality that I had. That group was special. I'm not sure what brought me around. I was just an immature kid. Somehow they saw something in me that I didn't. All of them played a part. They're my support group now. Terry Kelly, Sam's son-in-law, is my best friend. He gave me the first job I ever had. I did mean what I said earlier, I envy all of you the chance to be in your family business. Try not to lose sight of what you have. Being an entrepreneur can mean walking a long and lonely road…. I've talked enough. I better get things cleaned up."

We offered to help, but Mike wouldn't hear of it. Donna and I talked on for another two hours until we were too tired to continue. Most of the time we talked about her startup years, the ten long years it took her to become an overnight success. Right after her divorce she enrolled at George Brown College in the fashion design course. That had always been her interest. Donna had taken classical studies at university because her parents insisted that she needed a university degree. College wasn't good enough. This time she made her own decision and never looked back. It had been hard work but she enjoyed it from day one.

As far as the current state of her business she didn't say much about her daughters, but she really lit up about her overseas trips.

It had been a challenge to find reliable suppliers but she had several now. She showed me the Facebook page of her favourite supplier in India. The factory was owned and managed by an attractive middle-aged woman. That was an eye opener. I didn't expect female owners in India.

"Revathi has a thirst for knowledge and more determination than any man I know. She's a real entrepreneur and a great example of what Sam means when he talks about unleashing entrepreneurial talent around the world. Her factory is immaculate and her workers are content. Her product is consistent. She's a great lady — full of ideas and very determined."

That night I couldn't sleep. Was all this talk in the sessions making me think that I had more ability than I really had? Mike's words kept coming back to me: "don't lose sight of what you have." But I also kept seeing in my mind the picture of that Indian woman with the contented smile on her face. As Donna had said, a genuine entrepreneur. But not a family one; it turned out that her husband assisted her from time to time by travelling with her, but that was the extent of his involvement. As Donna pointed out: "Much as Sunjay would like to tell Revathi what do, she has no patience with his interference in her business. The boundaries are very clear."

The thought of that kind of independence was appealing. If I could only find a way, an opportunity that made sense, maybe I could discover that same contentment. If I couldn't resolve my family issues, was I brave enough to start on my own? And where would that idea lead? It was a sleepless night.

CHAPTER SIX

Is Talent Compromised?

Day Three.

We were settling in, totally comfortable with the format and beginning to relate to each other. Steve hadn't returned the night before. When he did show up at 2:30 that afternoon, he looked like death warmed over and remained fairly subdued throughout the session. In contrast Sam appeared well rested and relaxed. He even started with a personal observation, which was a rarity.

"I've missed this environment. The web broadens the reach but it weakens the connection. I didn't have the same feel for any of you from the webcasts that I used to get in my sessions, but I'm sensing it now."

Donna and I had discussed similar feelings the night before. The webcasts were great for information and both of us felt that Sam had connected with us, even in that context, but the open discussion and personal contact established a completely different relationship. It was the same with the online chats — great exchanges took place but they weren't as personal and felt less effective.

"We were rushing at the end yesterday, so there are a few suggestions I'd like to throw out that relate to leadership and to today's topic, which is talent. If you accept the premise that a family business can be a form of socialized entrepreneurship, how does that reality impact the entrepreneurial talent curve? Can you see any implications for the curve from the way some families operate?"

Normally Steve would have jumped in with his opinion at that point, but he was listless and pretty well out of commission for the moment. I decided to give it a shot.

"I can think of two effects and they relate back to Jeff's comments yesterday. One is that people on the left side of your talent curve, the part that has a lower level of entrepreneurial ability, may find opportunity in a family business that they wouldn't otherwise seek, get, or keep. The second is that people who are on the right side of your curve, injected into a family business, may not function well with the limitations they find and may strike out on their own. I mean, some won't since it really depends on the family culture, their perception of the opportunities, and whether or not their drive will be suppressed in the family interest. So in terms of the impact on a business we could be dealing with either unwarranted acceptance of inadequate talent or emotional rejection by significant talent, each from factors outside the business issues. Overall, I would say that the injection of family into a business situation can distort both business and personal choices."

Sam was pleased. "These types of instances certainly occur. Neither the business nor the family members who work there are fully subject to the vagaries of the market and can be over-protected or oversensitive. Personal factors can impact almost every decision related to talent, including leadership, strategy, remuneration, hiring, and firing. That impact can lead to sustaining incompetence or the loss of talent.

"I want us to revisit a story that we discussed in the online series. I told you about my first trip to South America. In South America the class system is still entrenched and it remains a major factor in the way business is conducted. While it's beginning to change, most firms are established family operations where participation is compulsory. Maintaining the wealth, stature, and power of the family are still the principal goals. Commerce is a means to that end. Traditionally it's been impossible to lead one of these companies as an outsider. The very best employees might make it to a management position, but never close to the top. This kind of exclusion based on family domination goes right back to the feudal system. It's a practice based solely on entitlement. Just look at the British royal family, where birth order constitutes the sole determinant of succession and it's almost impossible to opt out of the family business. Merit never comes into play. But at least they made the forward-thinking commitment to allow females to inherit the throne. Primogeniture is the right of the oldest son to inherit, and it is a deeply entrenched principle of human succession. The poor rural farm in India follows the same rule. The farm goes to the oldest. Other siblings are expected to work on the farm. If there are too many the younger ones leave and soon build up the levels of poverty in the cities. Competency does not come into question, just birth order.

"On that South American trip I saw some very capable business leaders but I also saw leaders with no interest or ability who reluctantly maintained positions in family empires. If they were lucky they were sustained by talented employees who covered up their lack of interest and ability. One of the most unusual experiences that I had was visiting the Novo Hamburgo area in Brazil where I met business owners who spoke German and looked and acted like Germans in every regard. Their families had settled there in the 1820s. The management and ownership of most of these companies was clearly Germanic, a legacy of lineage passed from one generation to the next. They had never assimilated. It was like someone had set down a piece of the fatherland an ocean away. It was eerie.

"I had a similar experience in Kolkata in India. There was an area in the city where the Hakka Chinese had settled generations ago. These people built family tanneries and leather goods firms behind high walls where they worked and lived. These quasi-foreigners still lived and worked in the Tangra region, an area of reclaimed land in the eastern part of the city. When I was in that area the entry doors, really large gates leading into these old industrial-residential complexes, were all painted red so you could tell the Chinese compounds from the Indian ones. This abnormality had been going on for over two hundred years with no assimilation. People worked in these businesses behind walls with no other option. Somehow they remained Chinese in every way, an island in a huge city of Bengali Indians. This isolation is finally changing because the old tanneries have been forced out of the city for pollution concerns.

"These two anecdotes are extreme illustrations of what can happen when family obligations and culture dominate the thinking of business owners. A family entity can sustain itself indefinitely in the face of extreme conditions and unique challenges. To some degree these abnormalities validate the strength of the family network, first in building and then in sustaining a business. Understand that in both cases these companies survived for generations following this approach, providing extreme examples that demonstrate that business can succeed when business principles are displaced by personal considerations. The talent pools were very limited and there were no personal options. Failure to integrate built huge loyalty within the smaller community at the expense of company and individual development. These pockets were truly communes, which leads back to the idea of socialized entrepreneurship — at least in the extreme. The main exception was that the leaders conducted business with outsiders but that contact was limited to a few owners who generally did the selling to the outside world."

It was always interesting when Sam drew on his travels and dealings abroad. Generally they were relevant and revealing.

"These radical situations illustrate what can happen, but in a more conventional setting entitlement manifests itself in many different ways. One startup I was involved with included two other partners. Together we purchased a mutual supplier of packaging materials that we all used. We weren't competitors but we knew each other as large customers of that company. Over the years we had attended quite a number of functions hosted by the supplier. Finding that we were like-minded on many issues, we had become personal friends along with the owner, who had decided to retire. He offered the company to the three of us as his first and best option. The decision was easy since the operation was profitable and acquiring it secured reliable supply for all of us. The synergies were promising. We were looking for a manager when one of the other partners suggested his brother, who worked for a large company. The brother was a mechanical engineer and seemed well qualified. After a rigorous interview process, we all agreed to take him on and gave him a 10 percent equity interest as an incentive to join us.

"In the midst of setting up the revised company structure he unnerved us all by asking quite innocently if he might be the president of the company as he had never been president of anything. None of us used titles in our respective businesses. After a lengthy group hesitation we agreed partially in deference to his brother, who we trusted. It proved to be a disaster. What he really wanted was his own company. It is one thing to *think* big but prematurely *acting* big can be problematic, and in this case it was. Our manager/minority shareholder had a large company attitude, expected unlimited resources, and took big company risks with small company assets. Bootstrapping was not in his vocabulary. *Thinking* big can lead to drive and accomplishment. *Acting* big can demotivate any team and result in paralysis. Aspiring to build something is not the same as assuming that you already have. It's a form of entitlement. Some people think being a business owner gives them prestige when it really just gives them responsibility and opportunity.

"None of us could relate to this approach. The rest of us had all sacrificed to establish our companies. It didn't take long for this fellow to alienate all of us, including his brother. He eventually owned the company. We just couldn't work with him, so he bought us out one by one. Ultimately, he lost all of us as customers as well and eventually went bankrupt. That fellow felt entitled and took advantage of his brother and the rest of us. None of us would have partnered with him or given him the title of president had it not been for the family relationship. His business opportunity didn't evolve from merit, he was just a family opportunist and he squandered his chance. There are tons of these freeloaders out there, maybe even in your own families."

Sam looked up to see if we were paying attention, which gave Donna a chance to ask a question.

"I'm glad you mentioned that last experience, Sam. Family businesses seem to end up in feuds and dismissals beyond the norm. I think it's because issues get suppressed to the point that they can't be any longer, leading to an explosion that's destructive. Issues like entitlement and nepotism are deadly. I worry about that a lot. I believe that my daughters pull their weight but I have lost at least two good hires because of the perception that any future would be limited. I find it ironic that while I've been fighting the glass ceiling all my life I've created the perception of a more tangible barrier within my own company."

Sam smiled but shook his head. "You're right about explosions and overreactions. I've seen some crazy disputes happen, rooted in dysfunctional relationships. An older gentleman who was a good customer of mine had a wool-dying factory in a small town located in tourist country. He opened an outlet store selling a full range of woollen goods and did spectacular business in the summer, which was off-season for his product line, but tourists loved his products. His wife and daughter were involved in purchasing various items from outside suppliers and merchandising the store. It was a captivating story about family, located in their old factory building, decorated with antiques and seething with character. Then the daughter got married. The father just didn't connect with his new son-in-law and refused to bring him into the business. Within two years a major feud had erupted. The younger couple retaliated by opening a competing store. Bear in mind this was in a town of fifteen hundred people that happened to be within reach of many summer tourists. Somehow they both succeeded, but the father — who I always felt was a generous, kind man — lost his only child to competition. They never reconciled and he left his business to the grandchildren. The stores have actually now been consolidated under the third generation. But it was a travesty and such a personal price to pay."

That anecdote was alarming. I was stunned but still had a question. "You're not making a very good case for family business at all, Sam. Do you have anything positive to say?"

Sam laughed out loud.

"These things don't happen every time. We're discussing pitfalls that are specific to family businesses, but they are not inevitable by any means. Families unite to provide platforms and opportunity for many capable people who would struggle otherwise. Some of them deserve it, others not so much. We know small enterprises can and do grow into national and international businesses. They create jobs where big business doesn't and they are the source for what becomes big business. The family unit does provide an incomparable support network for startups. But these drawbacks we've been discussing still exist and they must be managed. Companies that grow into significant entities wrestle these issues to the ground. For example, the DuPont clan, who created a substantial industrial empire, gave their own family members the chance to lead, but if they didn't demonstrate clear ability within the first five or six years that they could become a top level executive, they were shunted out of the company within the next ten years. The decision was made early based on proven potential. Opportunity was guaranteed, but merit ruled the day. There was pressure to produce or leave. That family retained leadership of the firm for more than 150 years. Non-family members who were in key positions were not given the highest level jobs, but they were given pseudo-stock that gave them profits and capital gains without diluting the ownership of the company. There was an impenetrable ceiling, as Donna described it, but the owners found other ways to compensate vital players, allowing them to attract and keep high-level talent. Most employees are motivated by reward. Unlike the family entrepreneurs who have been entrusted with preserving the entity itself as well as the image of the company, the majority of employees want above-average remuneration, job stability, and reasonable opportunity."

Donna was paying close attention to the DuPont story. Apparently finding and keeping talent was a real issue for her.

Finally Steve made his first comment of the day. "I have a real issue with entitlement. It's been building up and I don't want it to end in a feud. Donna's right, at least in my case. I've been suppressing my frustration and I'm ready to explode. My sister always felt that half the business should be hers. My dad ducked the succession issue so his will gave her what she wanted, but it's driving me crazy. It's not the money. I have the vision and the training to drive this business but I can't accept the difference between 'my business' and 'our business.' That's my issue, Sam. You know it from my application. My brother-in-law's a good guy, but I didn't choose him for a partner, my sister did."

Steve looked relieved to get his issue out in the open, but after an awkward pause Sam decided to wrap things up for the day.

"I still need to test some of my premises for the book with you. We missed last night so I have two for you today. Remember, these are for a book based primarily on our first webcast series. So I'm looking for thought-provoking ideas such as: 'Entrepreneurship is a life philosophy founded on opportunity, fuelled by determination, and focused on results.' Think about that from your perspective and experience then consider this second guideline: 'We only fail when we give up. Setbacks are just part of the learning curve on the road to success.' So I'd appreciate your feedback tomorrow and have a good night."

As we left Sam settled into an animated conversation with Steve.

CHAPTER SEVEN

A Less Stormy Night

Mike brought out platters of barbecued burgers and sausages, along with some fresh-baked cookies to serve with the coffee. It seemed like all four of us were staying in for the night. However, the whole idea of the camaraderie of the Brewhaha was drifting away, lost in the melodrama of personal issues. Steve had returned from his talk with Sam, so I spoke up.

"All right Steve, you opened the flood gates so let's talk about your frustration. Is it more with your sister or your brother-in-law?"

Steve looked up from his high-test espresso, showing a little more energy that he had all afternoon. He actually smiled. "I don't suppose I'm the only one here with issues. I think that's the prime reason we were picked. Isn't it Mike?"

Mike couldn't stop from smiling as well. "Tim and Sam chose the four of you. I didn't have anything to do with it. But from what I've overheard the selections were all about what direction the Family Entrepreneur sessions would take. Tim wanted it more focused on people considering starting a family business. Sam wanted to focus on people already committed and dealing with frustrations within that business setting. There's room for both. Tim was focused on the startup phase while Sam was more interesting in how these companies mature. Tim saw this as a

completely independent series. Sam wanted it to be a continua-
tion from the first round. I guess Sam won out. The last thing Sam
wanted to do was discourage people from starting a family-based
business. He thinks family support is one of the most effective
platforms for small business startups, at least in the traditional
economy. At the same time, he loves to see those businesses move
to the next level and even farther."

All four of us were paying close attention.

"I'd never seen the two of them argue like that before. This is
a business for Tim, so he was adamant — he felt confident they
would reach a larger audience his way. Sam was preoccupied with
improving the chances for an existing business. He finally won the
day when he told Tim that he was basically all wrong about the
business side. I think the exact quote was 'You idiot. Can't you see
this means two seminars instead of one for anyone who wants to
follow the program? That's not why I want to do it this way, but don't
worry, you'll make more money!' That settled it. They both started
laughing and as far as I know they've been in agreement since."

Knowing Sam it made sense. He always seemed to know
where he was going even when he meandered through a maze
of anecdotes. In our sessions he fostered the feeling that we were
creating this new series together, but were we? Well, if the program was focused on solving problems within a family business
we were all supposed to be problem solvers. So I tried again.

"So Steve, since we all have issues, what's your real problem?"

"I'm part of the problem. My sister's the other part. My brother-
in-law Dave is caught in the middle. I wasn't the only one who grew
up inside my dad's business. My sister and I both worked there all
the way through school. I took engineering followed by an MBA.
My sister is a pharmacist but she knows more about our operation
than her husband and has some pretty rigid views. Frankly, she's
still fighting my dad's battles for him. Like my dad she wanted to
establish a niche for high-quality fabricated products and keep
buying our stones from Italy. I wanted to focus on volume and

distribution from India with less emphasis on our own fabricating. We were into India early and I wanted to capitalize on the relationships we were making. I don't know, maybe it's the MBA mentality that bigger is better. I was really tempted to stay out of the business and head off to investment banking, but guilt and duty made me stay. I guess that's the root of my problem. I want to use the business as a platform to build something more significant, something that challenges me more beyond making a profit. My sister wants to protect my dad's legacy. I get it, but today's economy is all about change and scale of operation. We'll never agree."

Donna had a tear in her eye. "I can almost see this happening in my business. The concept was mine. I have two daughters. I can see this type of division on the horizon."

The problem was the polar opposite of mine. Steve's sister had shares, even though she wasn't active in the business. My brothers largely ignored me despite my contributions. I tried to ignore this irony for now and focus on Steve. Before I could say anything Jeff spoke up.

"You're not helping me, Steve. I'm much more concerned about my siblings than my father. They're younger than I am and I have no idea what their business interests are, what their strengths are, or if I can even work with them. I don't think they know themselves. This is exactly what has me nervous. Why didn't you buy your sister out after your father died?"

Steve seemed miffed at the suggestion. "The will was explicit: we're allowed to sell the company but otherwise we have to maintain the partnership. Neither of us is allowed to buy the other out. Call it control from the grave. The idea was that as long as his business was profitable my father wanted us to share the rewards. I have no complaint with his wishes — the will provides clearly for remuneration for management roles distinct from those of shareholders. He just didn't provide for dispute resolution. He should have set up a proper board but he died suddenly of a heart attack, leaving us stuck with a mess. That's one reason Dave wanted an active role. Paula had a solid career, plus Sam was right, it was logical and convenient to bring in Dave — maybe too convenient. But I didn't see it that way at the time. Even if I had tried I couldn't have blocked it."

Jeff was paying close attention. "So what's the dynamic like now? Are you constantly fighting? How do you make important decisions? Is the business suffering from gridlock?"

Steve shook his head quite vehemently.

"No, the company is doing well. We've had solid growth in both the top and bottom line. The housing industry is booming, especially the downtown condo market. Consumers are focused on location rather than sacrificing themselves to exhausting commutes. They often settle for smaller, more convenient spaces, but they want upgrades. The demand for marble and granite has been crazy. That's not the issue. The dilemma lies within me. It isn't enough for me. I don't want to be a mirror image of my dad or be my dad on a larger scale. I need to do more. I need to be different. Given the head start he gave me I need to be better."

It was great to see him open up like that. But I thought it was a mistake to give him off-the-cuff advice and push him in the wrong direction. God knows I was trying to make a similar decision myself, and I would probably discuss it with the others before we finished. For now I thought I should change the subject.

"It sounds to me that duty and guilt are playing a huge role for both you and your sister. Why don't we all think about this overnight? Maybe brainstorming with some outsiders like us can help you find a resolution. We're pretty much a neutral sounding board here. Anyway, we'd better make a quick review of Sam's postulates before we all go up for the evening."

This suggestion proved to be a good diversion. Steve started and was much more his old self as the four of us put Sam's ideas to the test. "I definitely agree that entrepreneurship is a philosophy, and he hit on the two biggest factors: opportunity and determination. Nothing happens without both of those factors. I guess I would like to call it a 'can-do' philosophy or mindset. You really have to welcome problems and relish their solution."

Everyone seemed to agree on that. Donna added her own perspective. "I like his second premise too. When I first started I was told repeatedly that failure was all right, even an essential part of the process. As far as I'm concerned failure sucks! I think the idea that it's necessary is just rationalization and a poor excuse for not managing the risk in your business. I know outside influences can change and take you down but even then you have to adapt, and quickly. He said it well. We will all make mistakes and hit setbacks but that only means failure if you stop and give up. If you adapt, all those negatives are just bumps in the road along the way, part of the learning curve. I like that!"

It seemed pretty obvious to me that all of us had become disciples of Sam.

"I guess we're not likely to disagree very much with any of Sam's ideas. We've pretty much embraced them all. He's preaching to the converted. But let's not tell him — I want to see what he's putting into the book. And besides, he always keeps us off balance. We'll just tell him we didn't have time to discuss it, or even better, let's not say anything." Everyone liked the idea of making Sam the one who was off balance for once.

CHAPTER EIGHT

The Team Within the Team

It worked. Sam's request for feedback the next morning was greeted with uncomfortable silence. Despite his obvious discomfort we all hung tough on our commitment to unnerve him. I almost blurted something out, but like everyone else I wanted to see how would react. Beyond a short initial hesitation he didn't. Stubborn. He just moved on.

"When we began this program I reminded you that we needed to focus on the entrepreneurial aspect of the family business. So based on our discussions to date, how does the family platform affect entrepreneurs?"

As the architect of stonewalling Sam, I was anxious to get past those first awkward moments so I answered immediately, with just a touch of sarcasm to encourage my cohorts.

"Well, Sam, as you know opportunity is the foundation of entrepreneurship." Jeff and Steve both chuckled out loud. "It seems to me that large numbers of people get their first exposure and maybe their only opportunity through a family company. We've talked about the many barriers to an entrepreneurial career, but this seems to be one area where barriers such as gender, funding, and even education can be overcome to give people a chance."

Sam didn't take the bait, ignoring my initial gambit related to his quote, and focused on the rest of my comment.

"Thanks, Mary. Many barriers are reduced in these companies. Women do get more opportunity. Funds are raised through collective effort and lack of education can be overcome by gaining experiences that others might not get. Any platform that brings more people into the fold is meaningful, but family support and encouragement may be the most common, even the most effective at overcoming a whole range of limitations, including personal inhibitions that hold people back from taking the leap into commitment. Even tech geniuses can find support for their initial concepts from their family members, whether financial or moral."

Jeff was sitting right beside me and let out an audible gasp at this. It wasn't the first time. But he didn't say a word. Instead Donna spoke out.

"On the negative side, I don't think the fundamental business problems are different, but the personal side is very challenging. We've talked about leadership and I know we're going into other areas soon. Overall, it seems to be that the problems are the same but the solutions are compromised by personal issues. You often emphasize the importance of balance, directing us not to become obsessed with our business to the detriment of our personal life. It seems for the family entrepreneur the two can merge so closely that values and decisions are blurred. The larger the entrepreneur builds that business, the more limitations emerge."

Sam appeared relaxed, well past any sense of frustration at our lack of response earlier.

"That's what this program needs to define. How do we find the right solutions for a growing business without ignoring the reality of the family platform? The more effectively I can get this across the better prepared these hardcore entrepreneurs will be and the better solutions they will find. They can't all follow models like the DuPont's, but they can customize their own solutions.

That's my goal — to make sure they don't get mired in predictable issues that can limit the business and damage the family."

Steve added something from his perspective. "There is something to be said for growing up in the culture of a family enterprise. You see the fundamental needs such as determination and problem-solving firsthand. I was certainly nurtured into an entrepreneurial lifestyle. The best thing is that I could either embrace it or reject it. My dad's success left me opportunity in several forms — a business to continue and an education, to choose a different path. Either way, the barriers that suppress entrepreneurship were pretty much removed for me. Even with education, a lot of people never understand the entrepreneurial option. The MBA program pushed me toward a career as an executive with a large business, not toward entrepreneurship."

I had a different thought. "One other potential negative is the preoccupation with protecting family assets and reputation. In a lot of cases this must make the management more risk averse and less open to innovation, so while they are motivated and committed to keep the company successful, conservative management could limit the potential of the company or even bring about its demise."

Sam was now in his element. "Good stuff. It is another contradiction about family entrepreneurs — there is some tendency to protect the status quo, a reluctance to disrupt what has been built, yet they've also been indoctrinated to entrepreneurial philosophy, focused on challenging the status quo. Steve and his sister reflect near polar opposites of these influences. However, I still want to defer any discussion of Steve's problem for now. We're going to continue to analyze other fundamental differences that affect leaders within a family entrepreneurship over the next few days. For today we're going to focus on team building. How does this distinct environment impact building a successful team?"

"In any business we're guilty of hiring for convenience," Donna said. "I've done it. It's tempting to look for the quick fix. Need means now, and it's not the best way to build the most effective team. That tendency is magnified in the family business. There's pressure to give family the first opportunity. Perhaps we see abilities in our family that don't exist, maybe we have wishful thinking. Or maybe we ignore the negatives more than we should out of a sense of duty. Once you've introduced family, there's a tendency to bring in even more. These are people you trust even when you shouldn't, and there's comfort in that. I suppose this inclination can lead to misplaced loyalty at both ends."

I could certainly relate to that — loyalty and duty were huge factors for me, overriding personal goals or wishes.

"I'm one of those convenient hires," I commented, "but I think that worked out pretty well for the company. I'm not sure that it worked out as well for me. When a company is small, loyalty and trust are major issues. If the leader is strong he can drag his family-based team along to become more successful. Once the company grows larger and you have to find talent that compliments the family group from outside, a whole range of issues comes out. I don't know how many times I've been asked by job applicants if there was real opportunity in our business. Nepotism, whether real or perceived, can undermine your ability to hire."

Steve seemed to agree. "Too many sympathy jobs are given out to family members. A bad hire is like a bad apple, it brings rot into the equation. I once gave a cousin a job because he was unemployed for over a year. It was partly bad luck, but he was unemployed for a reason. He had an inflated opinion of his abilities and the sense of entitlement he felt as part of my family magnified it. He just worked in the warehouse but I almost lost all of my core staff over his attitude. Luckily one of our oldest employees told me what was going on. I paid the cousin out for six months. Of course, that was more than I had to pay, but even that wasn't enough. He still complains about it at every family function. Bad hires can be a cancer and bad family hires are the worst."

Jeff finally had something meaningful to say. "We all know that diversity of skills is a major factor in assembling your team.

All family members are not clones, but duplication of strengths is more likely. To build a strong team you need opposites that can adjust to the company culture. That has to be much harder to do in a family-led scenario. Usually there are too many bosses or people who think they're bosses. That has to limit the talent pool available. Some people won't even consider a job in that environment. You mentioned that in one of your early businesses you often hired relatives of existing employees. That seems like a nightmare to me, like it would just magnify some of the problems that Mary and Steve outlined."

"You're right, it could make things worse," Sam replied. "We hired that way in a manufacturing company. We had fairly extensive in-house training programs and we also brought in outside consultants to train in skilled areas. There is a danger of assuming that if the existing employee is teachable and has a good work ethic that these traits extend to his brother or sister. Often they do, sometimes they don't. As Steve said, getting rid of a bad hire is worse in this situation, although the good employee is often relieved to see a relative who is not performing leave. Regardless, we developed some excellent team players from hiring on that basis. Some of them became supervisors and leaders as we evolved. If family ties are the only criteria, it's often a mistake. If they're part of your full assessment, they can give you some valuable insight."

This hiring practice was still bothering Jeff. "Don't you think the success of this approach depends on the scale of the operation? Also how scalable it may become? At some point this kind of sub-culture has to become a limitation. Potentially you're talking about a paternalistic organization where the leader is like the Godfather and everyone else follows his lead. I can't see this producing an effective team."

Sam did not totally disagree. "You're right, but you're also pre-judging the situation and assuming that these connected people can't grow and evolve with the business. That's why I mentioned outside training programs as well as a complete assessment of their potential. No one should get a key role in your team based on his connections, but it happens everywhere, and unfortunately, too often in the family operation. At the same time, if you can find loyalty and trust combined with ability and drive, that's the person you do want for your team. There's no replacement for a thorough screening and good judgement."

I wanted to ask something that pertained to me, but decided to bury it in a more general question. "That still doesn't answer how you attract talent that has no relationship to anyone within the organization. We use the word disruption a lot. But no matter how entrepreneurial a family company is, the disruptors need to be disrupted. Besides that, if you do attract good talent how do you keep it if upward mobility is blocked by family management?"

I was part of the family but I was still blocked at a lower tier by my gender. This was a very real problem for me. I was facing three choices: lead my brothers to a solution, follow the party line out of duty, or move on to something else. I was looking to Sam for a path to follow and he knew it. No one else in the room could connect the dots.

"Getting good people is easier than keeping them. If your company is on the rise and doing interesting things you will attract talent. The expectations you create at the time of hiring will play a major role in their job satisfaction. I'm a huge believer in pseudo shareholdings — some form of effective profit sharing that the owners can't or don't manipulate. Strategic involvement is critical for top talent. Top-down management dominated by the family better be brilliant or it will create resentment. If duty and obligation are the burdens of family members, then resentment and complaint are the millstones of outsiders. As far as keeping good people goes, creating effective involvement and rewards are the key. Beyond that it's incumbent on the employee to speak up. If he or she likes the company they have nothing to lose by pointing out the issue. No effective leader wants to lose talent. If you think the answer is no, you have nothing to lose and you might as well ask the question. After an open discussion, you'll know what to do."

That last was meant for me. If I loved the company, which I did, and the status quo was unacceptable, which it was, then try to change the status quo. In my own words "disrupt the disruptors." My brothers might be shocked but the ball would be in their court. No one else in the room realized how personal that answer was to me but it crystallized my thinking. I sat there a little dazed while the discussion continued. When I tuned back in, Jeff and Steve were in the midst of a heated discussion about Sam's last comments. Steve was almost shouting.

"I can't help it if you disagree, Jeff. The reality is that in most family businesses there's us and there's them, those on the inside and those on the outside. If you're one of us you hear all the informal deliberations that go on outside of work. That's how strategy evolves. The family is always a social unit and a hard one to crack unless you marry in like my brother-in-law. Even then there're no guarantees."

Jeff wasn't buying it. "You know I'm no big fan of being in any family business, but I think it boils down to leadership. You can't create a scalable business strictly on the back of family talent — not today. If you want family members included it takes leadership to get them in the right role and to make sure that outside talent reaches its potential or you'll lose them and limit the business in the process. If you're saying family business should level off and just meet the family needs rather than the business needs, you may be right and you may not even need outside talent. But that doesn't make you an effective entrepreneur in my book. I loved Sam's first program because it taught me that there's a solution to every problem and you, the entrepreneur, have to be committed to discover it. Finding and keeping outside talent is a solvable problem, at least within the context of a thriving business that needs outside influence."

Sam was enjoying the intensity of the exchange, especially seeing Jeff taking a positive stance on any aspect of the family enterprise. He seemed willing to let them continue but the brief dispute faded as fast as it erupted. Sam wasn't letting Jeff off easily.

"Interesting that you would take that position, Jeff. Basically you believe that family members can be effective without blocking outsiders from advancing."

Jeff looked embarrassed. Logic had overcome the emotion of his previous inflexible position. It was the first semi-positive thing he had said so far and Sam could not let it pass.

"I suppose not, Sam. By and large I support what you said earlier. These problems are still business issues, even if they're caused by family involvement. If we stay entrepreneurial the problems will be solved. A good leader will build his team using the best talent available. Family may be the tiebreaker, but it can't be the main factor."

Sam was beaming. Jeff was a skeptic, so his involvement was a positive note to end the session, and it was already after five o'clock.

"Thanks, Jeff. I know that concession didn't come easily. I have two more paradigms for you to consider tonight. If you don't comment back I'll just conclude that you approve."

Damn, it was tough to stay one up on Sam.

"These two are related: First 'Having ideas makes you a dreamer. Making them happen confirms you as an entrepreneur,' and, secondly, 'Entrepreneurs love the process more than the project.' There's some things for you to think about in your massive amount of free time. Have a good night."

CHAPTER NINE

Our Own Teamwork

Everyone moved directly to the lounge. Our little gambit to out-manoeuvre Sam had united us, even if he pretty well ignored it. Shared laughter was a refreshing change. Mike surprised us with homemade Chelsea buns that he had learned to make at his café up north. Tim hadn't been around the last two days so Mike was working without help to record the discussion and catch all the highlights. I'm not sure when or how he did the baking. These social times following Sam's presentation were an effective way to bond the group together — even the online chats worked in the same way. As Mike passed the Chelsea around, I asked him about Sam.

"Why doesn't he ever join us for coffee?"

Mike shrugged.

"My guess is that he wants to see every group unite rather than just convert people to his ideas. His intent is to be thought provoking and leave you with lots to talk about. It works every time; each group takes on its own personality and most of them stay connected."

Our group was finally coming together. The other three were busy debating Sam's last two points. None of us were serial entrepreneurs, at least not yet, since the four of us were still in our first entrepreneurial situation. Only Donna had actually done a startup. She was describing her experience to the others.

"I think I understand what he means; if you can survive one startup, than you're ready and able to do it again. The process is like a runner's high — being in the midst of it is exciting and you feed off the energy of the action. It's like a revolving door of problems and decisions that only you can handle. I definitely fed off the adrenaline of being in the eye of the hurricane. I would love to do it again for a completely different project. Maybe I will yet."

Steve was almost spellbound. "That's exactly what I'm looking for," he said. "I want to be 'the guy' not 'the son of the guy.' I want to be in the centre of the action stemming from my ideas, my commitment, working with my team to make my project happen. Then I want to do it again and again. It's nothing to do with ego or money. It's about the challenge."

I think I was starting to get it as well, but I had doubts that I would ever capture that feeling of challenge and accomplishment working with my brothers. They had it but they didn't include me as part of it. My role in their eyes was clerical and they saw me as replaceable, but I knew better. I had lots of scope for leadership and innovation that they chose to ignore. Maybe this week was helping me resolve my issues after all. I would take the cue from Sam and confront them, but my reluctance to leave out of duty was fading away in the excitement of contemplating my own startup. Then Jeff said something else that didn't quite compute.

"There's really nothing like it; pure joy that gives you a complete sense of true independence to sink or swim, to succeed or fail. But when you're in the midst of it there is no sense of possible failure. That feeling of entrepreneurial infallibility that Sam talks about is very real and it is an emotional high. You just can't let it dominate your decisions or you will overshoot the mark out of arrogance."

Steve was staring at Jeff in total disbelief. "What are you talking about? You haven't even decided to go into your dad's business yet. What do you know about leading a startup? You're not even wet behind the ears."

I was actually sorry for Jeff. These two kept having minor dust-ups. "Leave him alone, Steve. Maybe that's what he really wants: to run his own show, not to join his dad. You should certainly understand that."

Steve glared at me for a moment and then burst out laughing. "You're right, Mary. I guess we all have the same dream. We've proven we can make things happen, now we want to do it on our own to prove we can. That's a good thing. Is that what you want too?"

"I'm not sure for me. Not yet. But there's no doubt about you or Donna, and maybe not even Jeff."

The rest of the night was filled with entrepreneurial speculation. Donna had ideas for three or four other businesses, all of them online retail in different forms. Steve was intent on building a real estate empire focused on redevelopment consistent with the provincial policy of infilling. He had been researching opportunities in more remote urban areas where there were a lot of old stone industrial sites that were vacant. He was intent on following an established practice in the city of converting outdated industrial properties to residential use and had found several ideal sites that were stagnating with existing infrastructure in place. At least he thought they were ideal. I felt the risk was in the timing more than the concept. Remote areas could take a long time. Jeff stayed quiet, taking it all in. It seemed that Steve's outburst had deflated him.

As for me, my mind was whirling around, debating the pros and cons of starting new or proving my value and staying in my business within a business, which I now recognized gave me that same entrepreneurial buzz that Donna had described earlier. Dinner proved to be the Chelsea buns and several coffees before we all went up around ten o'clock. Whatever the reason, I hardly slept that night as my brain continued to spin with the possibilities: all good for once.

CHAPTER TEN

Controlled or Controlling?

Tired or not, my days were picking up speed as the week evolved. My mornings and early afternoons were jam-packed with business issues. It was already Thursday and three o'clock seemed more like lunchtime. I had missed lunch for the third time that week. There was ongoing chatter as I entered the meeting room late for the first time. Donna was talking to Tim, who was back that day, while Mike was engaged with some problem with his camera and Steve and Jeff were yet again debating some contentious issue. Sam was reading from a few typewritten sheets at the front of the room, maybe a draft of his book, because at second glance the bundle looked quite thick. Once I took my seat, he stuffed them in his briefcase and was ready to start.

"I thought I'd expand on a comment that Mary made yesterday about the family business becoming so focused on reputation and preserving assets that it could become too conservative, to the detriment of both the business and the family. For a short while in between businesses I developed an agency/trading company. This was in the mid-1990s, right after NAFTA was passed. I was intrigued by Mexico and decided to explore the possibilities there. As you know, I dealt extensively with Brazil and Argentina earlier in my career and I expected a similar market. On the surface there were quite a few common practices, but the culture was very different. Most of the businesses I dealt with were family-owned companies that went back several generations. The factories were modern and the products were quite well made. On the surface they looked well prepared to take advantage of NAFTA. They had a huge labour advantage and easy access to the largest consumer market in the world.

"The problem was the business culture. I made some great introductions and secured several sizable contracts that were never delivered. Communication was absurd, primarily at their convenience. The people were exceptionally nice and gracious, but their business goals were completely subjugated to personal needs. The reality was that these people were rich and living well off their established business activity. They lacked ambition and were more than content with the status quo. Mexico is a prime example of how entry barriers to entrepreneurship reduce competition and limit the drive of an economy. There was so much undeveloped potential and no engine of determination to drive improvement. The *mañana* mentality was a real phenomenon. I was told very early that when a Mexican said *mañana* it didn't mean 'tomorrow,' it meant 'not today.' Trying to get answers drove me to abstraction. There was no sense of priorities and no value put on new business.

"I should have clued in on my first day. My contact, who was well educated and had worked in Japan for several years, was supposed to pick me up at 10:00 a.m., which is when the offices generally opened. He arrived at 11:15. Sensing I was upset he informed me that 'when a Mexican says he is going to pick you up at ten, all that means is that he won't pick you up before ten.' His rationalization was that Mexicans were happy and didn't get stressed. That was true for the privileged class. With limited or no upward mobility there was a distinct absence of drive that was, and still is, disturbing. Of course, there are tons of implications, including the immigration issues that transferred lack of opportunity into illegal entry to the U.S. That was the only hope for the poor to improve themselves. The immigration problem was a double-edged sword: lack of opportunity at home compounded by a toothless border that allowed illegal immigrants to cross and find jobs on the American side.

"This dichotomy, an apparent contradiction, was reinforced when I was doing business in Chicago around the same time. It was a Thursday morning and I was visiting a friend's office when the factory was raided. Over thirty Mexican workers whose papers were not legal were removed and taken by bus back to Mexico. There was relatively little disruption. Everyone from my friend to the management to the plant workers to the federal employees conducting the raid, even those being removed, took things in stride. I was in a state of shock. When I asked my friend if this would set him back since he was losing over thirty workers out of a staff of maybe a 125, he shrugged and said 'Almost all of them will be back to work on Monday morning. Then we won't be raided for another year or more.' There were no penalties. The system was a farce.

"So there you have both sides of the Mexican situation. Limiting opportunity on the Mexican side and abusing it on the American side. Getting back to Mary's point she's right. Conservative family management in the extreme can kill entrepreneurship, limit the business, and damage individual economies. It's one more reason we do need governments to remove the barriers that suppress entrepreneurs around the world."

Steve was anxious to comment. "Are you saying that the family business is a barrier to progress?"

Sam was pacing across the front of the room and wheeled around to look directly at Steve. "Of course not. Things are much more complicated than that. I've just pointed out a scenario that proves Mary's point. If you're part of a culture that protects the status quo, then conservatism creeps into your management style and can actually dominate it. Once you have a business in that environment you are prone to give all upper-level positions to family and you become risk averse. If you want to take it farther, this narrative points out one of the flaws in our human character. Once we get ours, so to speak, we're not so concerned about others and we want to protect what we have. That's human nature based on greed. Right now we're on a road to gross inequality in the distribution of wealth and I'm worried about the consequences. Dominance of the world economy by big entities combined with little job stability and the potential suppression of individualism makes me worry that we could throw ourselves backwards into a modern feudal system, where those at the top are insulated from the rest of us who subsist with little or no hope for improvement. That's overstated, I'm sure, but I don't like where we're headed."

Silence filled the room.

Sam collected himself for a minute, and then directed the subject back to our program with no further comment about the future. "So today we're going to review controls. They're critical in any owner-operated business, but somewhat different in the family-owned scenario. What do you think?"

There was some reluctance to speak up. Sam's earlier passion had created apprehension. When we hit these bumps in the road, it seemed to fall to me to break the ice, so I tried.

"Informality," I muttered. "There's so much integration of the business with family interaction, at least during the startup phase, that there is a strong hands-on management approach. Bootstrapping is a way of life; live within your means. The family's cash flow and the business's cash flow are one and the same. That's true for most startups, but it's spread across a broader group in a family platform. That's exactly what I found in my brother's business when I joined him. He didn't understand accounting, but he maintained tight control over his cash. He had to because that's how he fed his family. Strategy was informal as well. At first he bounced ideas off his wife and my father at night when he went home. Later he and my brother would do the same thing over a beer at the end of the day. Basically what controls were in place were informal."

"How did that make you feel and how has the company evolved?" Donna asked.

"I didn't like it. Long before I took Sam's web program I strived to put in controls. From operating budgets to job descriptions to plans and projections, I still push my brothers to establish controls. I've developed budgets based on history. The two of them hate to look at them, but they do provide a framework. When there's a trend moving us off target they listen and react, which is great. They do have their own system of accountability in the field, but it's largely a hands-on approach since every crew is under their direct control."

Sam was engaged in my account of our business.

"That's a fairly good summary of what tends to happen. The family leaders can easily develop tunnel vision. As far as strategy goes, the more family members involved the more sporadic the direction of the business can become. Everyone has an opinion. Management by committee is dangerous. Accountability can be sacrificed to family loyalty or mistakes can produce irrational arguments that lead to major rifts. Usually this happens because minor errors are ignored until the cumulative effect leads to an overreaction. In one of the companies I mentored I saw an unbelievable one-sided blow-up when one brother did literally nothing. It happened in a meeting in which a group of strategic partners were reviewing a project. The second brother desperately wanted to proceed with the project but couldn't without the involvement and support of all the potential partners. The first brother had some serious reservations and felt that the project was high risk. Rather than sink the project he stayed silent in the meeting, while the other partners basically trashed the idea as too risky. As far as the second brother was concerned this was simply a betrayal. He expected unconditional support, even if the project was dangerous.

"There was a steady stream of emails all generated in anger. The damage to the family relationship was permanent. It's the type of explosion that happens when family loyalty suppresses frustration until it's too late. That particular disagreement morphed into the next generation and the family split became entrenched. Families can provide a rock of support, but that same intransience can become a rock of resistance if things evolve the wrong way. Familiarity breeds contempt. It's no coincidence that the word 'familiar' derives from family."

Steve responded in a predictable and personal way. "I'm very concerned that I'm close to that kind of blow-up with my sister. I've been suppressing it since my father died and I don't think she has any idea. If I blow up she won't see it coming and it will be a disaster. My brother-in-law will be a casualty of war."

Sam looked concerned. "Steve, that's why we're here and why I agreed to do this program. Not for you specifically, but to define the challenges of being an entrepreneur in a family business so people are prepared to deal with them on a timely and effective basis. You haven't blown up yet and there are still ways to solve your problem. You can't keep denying it and you have to face it head-on as rationally as you can. Emotion can't be allowed to dominate the conversation."

Steve was barely hanging on by his fingernails. I wanted to help him. I felt sorry for him and for his sister. At least my frustration wasn't personal — not yet. Maybe this was another warning. Sam didn't dwell on the issue. Personal issues were generally downplayed during his sessions.

"Getting back to the problem of informality and the need for clearly stated controls, there's one solution that I recommended several times when I consulted family-owned businesses: bring in a chief financial officer or controller who is not a family member. This was always greeted with resistance, as trust is the guiding principle in a family business. The corollary of the premise that you can trust family is that you can't trust outsiders. Lack of opportunity may scare off outside talent, but mistrust compromises a whole range of hiring decisions for family entrepreneurs. There is no greater area of suspicion than the finances of the business, which are so closely tied to the financial well-being of the family. However, my experience refutes this flawed logic. Once a fully qualified financial manager is put in place the family managers come to rely on him and trust builds. Budgets are formulated. Results are monitored. Compensation is reviewed from a business perspective. Better tax planning exists. Questionable spending decisions are analyzed more carefully. If this person works out, as he or she should, it opens up possibilities for other outside hires because it demonstrates the need and benefits of specialized staff. I believe this is absolutely critical for the evolution and maturation of every family business. Mary, it sounds like you did many of these things for your brothers, but because you're an insider they've been taken for granted."

The discussion was more personal than I expected. It felt like Steve and I were kind of under a microscope. Sam continued moving in a slightly different direction.

"A financial controller can mitigate a lot of issues, not the least of which is ego. Ego is a danger for all entrepreneurs, but is somewhat worse in a family situation. This is a real threat when there are at least two generations involved and the older generation becomes preoccupied with leaving a legacy and/or consolidating a larger company to pass on to the next generation. If you combine this goal with a sense of entrepreneurial infallibility that comes with a long career as the boss, reinforced by automatic family respect and support, you have a recipe for disaster. Usually this takes the form of a large new project designed to endure. Costs are ignored to build a business monument. In the extreme we have the pyramids and the Taj Mahal to remind us that humans like to build lasting memorials. From a business point of view any major project that ignores cost control is a threat. A good controller can shepherd the company through a process that is very important on a personal level, under the umbrella of a realistic budget and a realistic time frame. Without this type of third-party influence the foundation of the business can be shaken by financial irresponsibility. I have seen at least three companies that had to be sold out from under the next generation because of a career-ending project for the founder that undermined the financial strength of the company."

Sam checked his watch. It was just five o'clock.

"Since tomorrow's Saturday and you have Sunday free, I suggest we meet at ten o'clock and wind up by noon. I presume you'll be leaving, but you don't have to check out. We have the rooms booked right through to next weekend. However, I'm not letting you get away without some more pearls of wisdom to consider. First: 'A plan is one possible outcome. The planning process provides a framework to anticipate and adjust.' That's one you shouldn't ignore. For my second one: 'Growth provides the life's blood for entrepreneurs, but it can act like a python, exhausting your strengths and crushing your ability to survive.' I don't think you can ignore that one either since growth is such a temptation for all of us. Anyway, have a good night."

CHAPTER ELEVEN

Birthday Blues

When we reached the lounge Mike had a birthday cake for me with thirty-two candles blazing away. In the rush to get everything done that morning, I'd forgotten it was November 8. After the most horrid version of "Happy Birthday" I could remember hearing, Tim broke out a relatively sweet German Riesling, which happened to be one of my favourites. Steve left for a few minutes only to reappear with a bottle of Glenfiddich 18, a great bottle of single malt scotch that he declared to be eminently more suitable for a birthday celebration. Apparently Tim and Donna agreed because the three of them were soon sipping scotch on the rocks. Jeff joined me with the Riesling. Mike didn't drink. Before long the level of conversation was on the rise.

All of us wanted to know if Tim was pleased with the program so far. He had been guarded in his comments all week, but apparently the scotch loosened his tongue.

"Sam rarely disappoints and he's gotten better at drawing out his class. When we first met he used to do most of the talking in these sessions. I would say close to 80 percent. He always got us talking but used more anecdotes. This time he has all of you engaged and he's made you an active part of the teaching process. He and I have debated whether to use these sessions as a prototype for future webcasts or to just offer it as a program for view that covers the basis of family entrepreneurship that we sell as-is for people to download. Sam prefers new interactive webinars with fresh groups and their own problems. Of course that's more expensive and time-consuming, but right now we do have several hundred people who have applied for this program without us making any details available. Over the past four years Sam's basic webcasts on entrepreneurship have been broadcasted to over 2,500 people. We limit the online class to fifty each time, so he's done the series over fifty times. I don't think he can sustain the pace, which is why I've suggested that we record a course with a solid group like you that we can blast as needed, perhaps with Sam offering a Q and A online after each session or an email-based exchange with him. If we don't do that he's going to have to increase the number of people in each session. He'll resist that. Sam studies the background of every participant and tries to direct some comments to every one of them over the course of the session. You've all experienced his webcast and now his personal program. How do you feel about it?"

I was surprised and so were the others. The possibility of broadcasting our private seminar hadn't been discussed. We were here to resolve our problems, not expose them in any public way. Steve spoke up about his concerns, which were similar to mine.

"You should have told us. I know you told me you were recording but I thought that was just for you and Sam to review, not for publication, so to speak. I said some things that I might not want to share publically."

Tim didn't argue.

"First of all, we might not even offer it as is, but if we decide to go in that direction you will all have to sign off on the final product, and there would be some reward every time we use it. On review if there are things you want removed we will either edit them out or ask you to re-record that portion with adjustments. But this is all premature because I have to convince Sam that this is the best approach. That won't happen until we all see the final product from these two weeks."

Tim's explanation seemed to mollify everyone. The scotch and the Riesling didn't hurt either. By this point we were all pretty mellow. Before long Tim had to leave so he declined a third scotch. No one else did. As he left he assured us we needn't worry. He suggested that we discuss the idea next week with clearer heads.

After he left, we had Mike order us pizza since no one felt like driving or sitting in a restaurant. After the pizza arrived we broke up into two groups based on gender. The three guys wanted to watch a hockey game while Donna and I settled into a conversation about her business.

"Mary, what's your plan for tomorrow? Are you going home?" I had already decided that I'd just stay at the Mill. I didn't feel like bothering to go home for basically twenty four hours.

"I don't think so, Donna. It's not worth it for me. I'm thinking of just staying here."

Donna wouldn't hear of me being alone on my birthday weekend.

"You're not doing that on your birthday! Come to my place. I've got a nice condo right downtown on the Lakeshore. We can walk to Harbour Sixty and have a great meal. On Sunday I'd like to show you around my office. I know from our conversations that you're interested in the fashion business. C'mon, it'll be fun!"

Why not? I would only work if I stayed at the inn, and other than Mike everyone else was leaving.

"Okay. I think you've talked me into it."

We spent the next two hours sipping a second bottle of wine while the guys downgraded from scotch to beer, except for Mike, who was still abstaining. By the time the game was over it was eleven o'clock and I had a rudimentary idea of how Donna's business was structured, while she knew quite a bit more about my role and my frustrations. All of us were ready to collapse into bed. It was a good thing none of us had to drive. We hadn't given Sam's ideas the slightest bit of thought, and at that point none of us cared. It had been an interesting first week but all of us were ready for a break.

CHAPTER TWELVE

A Free-For-All

Sam showed up as fresh as could be while the rest of us dragged ourselves in bleary-eyed, coffees in hand. He had learned his lesson and didn't ask for any response about his growing list of entrepreneurial maxims. But he did throw us a different curve.

"Let's take a break from the family business today and get back to some basic entrepreneurship issues. Maybe I can slip in a few anecdotes to lighten your load; it looks like all of you could use that this morning. So why don't you ask the questions today — your choice, bring up any topic that you feel like. What do you say?"

That was an easy sell. All of us were in a better mood to listen than to deliberate over Sam's theories. As it turned out, Donna asked the perfect question to get Sam started.

"Three weeks ago Canada announced a free trade pact with Europe. When you add NAFTA into the mix we now have free trade agreements with forty-two countries. Sam, in the past you've given us anecdotes about Asia and South America and yesterday Mexico, but other than generalities about your business you've said very little about North America or Europe. How about telling some experiences from there?"

Sam thought about it for a minute and then nodded his head.

"Well, I have told you many stories about running my various businesses here, but I guess I've never given you an overview of my experiences in each market. Let's start with Europe. My only real experience selling there was in the U.K. We actually started our own distribution company there that we operated with limited success for about ten years. Our products were quite unique, which we'd proved here and in the U.S. market, but the Brits were conservative and had the idea that anything from the 'colonies' must be inferior. We were supposed to supply them with raw materials, not advanced products. Overall I didn't find Europe to be as open to innovation, at least from the outside. Maybe they had been at the top of the heap for too long and were resistant to change even as they declined somewhat.

"The exception was Italy, which was flourishing with innovation both in product and in process. We bought machinery and some high-quality raw material in Italy. They had great concepts, but if you wanted the equipment to last you waited for the Germans to produce their rock-solid knockoffs of the Italian designs. The German machines lasted forever. The French were difficult and quite arrogant. I remember coming back from an international trade show with a French-Canadian businessman who spoke English with a fairly heavy accent. He was angry. He said, 'You know I do business all over North America and have many friends. No one has ever mocked my English, at least not to my face. Here they call me a 'Provencal' and laugh openly at my French.'

"On that same trip my partner and I arrived on a charter three days before the trade show started. There were several Americans on our flight who stayed in the same hotel. We used the three days to tour around Paris. Since we were from Canada we spoke adequate French to make ourselves understood and had been reluctantly accepted by the waiters in the Parisian restaurants. On the third night we met an American fellow who had been on our flight and was travelling alone. He practically begged us to take him with us for dinner. He couldn't speak a word of French and the waiters refused to speak English. He had eaten very little for three days. Of course, things have improved since the EU was formed, but the French are a special breed."

Sam was off and running and we were more than willing to listen. After a couple of sips from his water bottle he continued on.

"Canada was our first market and a very tough breeding ground. Our customers were demanding on quality and tough-as-nails on price. We were young and our competitors in English Canada had no intention of letting us into the club. That continued until we grew so big that they had to acknowledge us. We were selling specialty materials to manufacturers, so 95 percent of our business was in Ontario and Quebec. The Ontario market was tough for newcomers. The Quebec market was divided. We did very well with the Jewish-owned companies in Montreal. I made some very good friends there. I found them to be very innovative, so if your product was good they would use it. Price negotiations were always fun but they were fair. At first we couldn't penetrate the French-owned companies. Once we took on a very affable young French Canadian who was well liked and very hard working as our agent things improved. From that point on we grew with those companies as well.

"My first experience with U.S. companies was as a buyer looking for supply. In Canada we found ourselves closed off from many suppliers who gave us little encouragement and offered product at outrageous prices, threatened by the fact that we were developing new and innovative products that they were not making themselves. Remember, the two of us were just twenty-three, so hardly a threat to established companies. When we went to the States for the first time we found a completely different attitude. Canadian suppliers wouldn't give us the time of day but the reaction in the U.S was that it was great to see two young guys starting up in the industry. When we went to quite a large operation owned by a well-known national firm the vice-president of marketing spent the whole afternoon showing us around the plant, answering all of our questions patiently. When he found out that our wives were travelling with us he loaned us his key to the Boston Playboy Club and the four us had a lark going there. I learned a lot about entrepreneurship from the Americans.

"Several years later, in 1976, we had developed some different and fairly unique products to which no one else was paying attention. At the time the Canadian dollar was well above the U.S. dollar, so it was not a good time to try and sell into a very competitive U.S. market. Our banker told us we were wasting our time."

Sam had never before spoken about his experience as a Canadian selling into the U.S. market. All of our lives we'd been taught that it was critical for the Canadian dollar to be well below its U.S. counterpart. Parity was still considered a near disaster for the Canadian manufacturing sector. The prevailing wisdom forever had been that Canadian companies would lose their U.S. customers if parity lasted for any length of time. Was this reality or a reflection of our collective inferiority complex? Probably both. Still, to sell into that market with our dollar at a significant premium had to be a serious challenge. That was a fact of life. Apparently Sam had been up to the challenge.

"The U.S. market is anything but homogeneous. The best states for Canadians to deal in are generally the border states where the people have some knowledge of Canada. But let's not get ahead of the story. We were apprehensive. The prevailing wisdom was that Americans were extremely tough and would laugh us out of their office if we tried to sell to them. Later we had the common sense to recruit some very good U.S. agents, but at first we went in cold turkey. Our reality was completely different from the general perception. The big bad American businessman liked our product because it was different, and as long as they could make money on it they would pay our price. They told us openly that our product was unique and that's what they liked. Almost all of our accounts in the U.S. had started as family-owned manufacturing companies. In Canada our customers were much tougher and would never acknowledge the uniqueness of our product. The Americans were more entrepreneurial and only looked at what our product could do for them. It was an important lesson for me as an entrepreneur. It helped us grow the business in both countries because we had a better understanding of where our products stood in the marketplace. Some of my best times as an entrepreneur were spent with American designers, brainstorming what we could develop for them to stay ahead on trends. Creativity allowed us to do more than 50 percent of our business in the U.S. market.

"That's not to say those same customers wouldn't be tough on price if our product was the same as others. If products were interchangeable, they were relentless in beating you up on price. There was a premium for being better and different; but penalties for being the same or inferior. That's a valuable lesson for any entrepreneur. Being first can be difficult. You have to face a tough market and a hard sell for a product people don't recognize or understand. Making an established product different and better provides a more stable and predictable path to success. It's an important lesson for today's entrepreneurs, even the tech types. Quick example: coffee is not a new product and meeting over one isn't a new idea. Coffee houses were prominent in London and Vienna by 1650. So how do you explain the success of Tim Hortons and Starbucks? They have two new and different approaches to a very mature product and market; both prove the reward that comes from doing something better and different. Only a few of us combine innovation with entrepreneurship and become the first with some great commercial idea. But all of us have the chance of taking a good idea with a proven market and doing it better.

"If your product is the same as your competition, the only negotiable factor becomes price. I saw disturbing evidence of the damage that reliance on price competition can bring in both Korea and India later on in my career. In Korea I saw a brand-new plant that had been set up to make 5,000 pairs of white athletic shoes per day for a large U.S. marketer. The Korean company kept the business for two years before losing it to a competitor in Thailand for twenty cents a pair. The factory was like new, a modern ghost factory with no production. I saw the same thing in India in a leather garment factory. There sat the most modern equipment, all made in Germany, idle after only one year of getting the business from a large U.S. company. If you want to succeed in the U.S market you have to be innovative enough to distinguish your products and allow the customer to make his own premium or you have to be prepared to compete on price. There's no resting on your record. Being different today doesn't last long. With globalization, too often competition is boiling down to price. Falling behind is deadly. There is no such thing as customer loyalty. Marketing and branding are controlled by the U.S. seller. The production can be moved anywhere and often is. Unfortunately, other countries are following the same model.

"Research In Motion, the creator of BlackBerry, is a painful but perfect example. As long as their innovation stayed ahead of their competition, their product was embraced in the U.S market. As soon as they slipped behind they began to sink like a rock. It's a critical lesson for any company that hopes to succeed in the largest consumer market in the world or, increasingly, anywhere else. You have to be different and better and you have to stay ahead. The more we move toward a true global economy the more this is going to be our reality. The largest target market *will* change. India and China are growing consumer markets with huge numbers of eager potential consumers, but the reality of global competition will stay the same. That's why entrepreneurship and innovation are such keys to keeping individual companies and economies healthy. Governments know this. There is a developing battle to attract talent. Entrepreneurship is being emphasized in virtually every country. Huge companies can't move fast enough. Their growth depends more and more on acquisition. The entire world is becoming a competitive idea factory. It's a high-pressure environment, ideal for innovation and entrepreneurship but tough for stability and longevity."

We all had questions. Jeff went first.

"How does Canada fit into this fast-paced environment?"

Sam was pensive before he answered. After all, he was projecting our future.

"Canada has some strong pluses. But remember this is a dynamic situation. We have very substantial resources that are large relative to our population. We have a multi-cultural society that will help us develop key trading relationships as the strength of the world economy shifts. We have an effective immigration policy that focuses on bringing in talent. Our education system ranks well, but we are flirting with cutting our investments in that area, which is short-sighted. If we have to cut costs let's make sure we don't cut in critical areas that will undermine our competitiveness. We need to worry about our productivity and our dependence on the U.S. market. As a country and as independent companies we had better develop new trading partners, and fast! We have benefitted from the dominance of the West in the world economy. As that dwindles we will feel the pain. Overall, like everyone else, our future depends on seizing opportunity and making things happen before others can."

Steve was concerned. "It sounds like you feel the U.S. is in for a downward spiral. Do you feel the U.S. will stay dominant in the world economy?"

Sam smiled at the suggestion.

"I would never bet against our friends and neighbours. Americans are very entrepreneurial. That has not changed. American companies are international leaders and will stay so. The American consumer will have a rougher ride. The increasing discrepancy in the distribution of wealth concerns me. The political dysfunction bothers me even more since this is a time for leadership and sound decision making. As it stands,

Congress has no hope of making optimal decisions at such a critical time. The United States is facing an economic tipping point and there are huge implications for us and the rest of the world based on how they handle it."

Donna went next. "So far today you've focused primarily on Canada as an exporter. That's just one opportunity for entrepreneurs. As an importer I feel that globalization opens up terrific opportunities for small flexible businesses run by entrepreneurs like ourselves. What are your thoughts on that?"

"That's the real lesson that I've been trying to get across. All through my career I invested in visiting and understanding markets around the world. That investment of time led to many opportunities but most of all a better understanding of what was possible. You have to do the same. It's far more critical today because globalization is here to stay. The markets I've been describing are all in a state of change. You have to do your own assessment based specifically on your business and your willingness to pursue opportunity. Whatever you do, don't live in a cocoon."

It was my turn. This was not an area that my brothers would consider relevant, but it was. Many of our supplies were imported and the overall health of the Canadian economy was the major determinant of our business and critical for how we reinvested. Immigration was a major factor in the health of the Canadian real estate market. New home building was the major source of our growth.

"Sam, do you think that Canada will continue to follow an expansionary immigration policy in the face of all these global changes?"

This was somewhat of a change in direction, but Sam didn't seem to mind at all.

"I think so and I hope so. Canada is still a highly desirable place to live and the demographics establish a need for us to bring in younger people to whom we can offer real opportunity. This gives Canada some advantage in the worldwide competition to attract talent. Immigration at the levels we have relative to our population brings growth to our markets. Immigrants bring skills and find employment relatively quickly. They are entrepreneurial and soon become consumers and often job creators. As long as we maintain a relatively stable entry level each year they offer stimulus to our economy. Any business dependent on domestic consumption needs to pay close attention to immigration trends and policy."

The discussion offered a lot to absorb. It was a nice change of pace from the challenges of the family business. Sam didn't let us off without adding two more of his entrepreneurial principles.

"Before you leave here are my two thoughts of the day. First: 'Only one company can do things first. The broader, more enduring path to success is doing things better and different.' As for the second one, it goes 'Anticipation paves the road to solutions; preoccupation is a roadblock to achievement.' Both are relevant to our discussion this morning. Enjoy your weekend, brief as it is."

And with that dismissal we were on our way, ready and eager to have a break but stimulated by a provocative morning session.

CHAPTER THIRTEEN

A New Experience

The drive with Donna into Toronto was filled with conversation about Sam and speculation if at the end of our careers we would have the wealth of information and experiences that he had accumulated. Both of us agreed that was unlikely. It was a short trip, less than half an hour, since there was little or no traffic early on a Saturday afternoon. It was a beautiful Indian summer day and the view from Donna's apartment overlooking Lake Ontario was spectacular. We were close to the Toronto Islands and could see the last sailboats of the season getting the most out of the day. Strong westerly winds made the sailing a challenge and fun to watch, even from a distance. We spent the afternoon sipping wine on her balcony, totally relaxed. Donna had made a reservation at Harbour Sixty for seven o'clock, which meant we'd arrive after the hockey crowd left. Not too shabby; I could get used to the life-style. She clearly loved the vista from her condo.

"You should have seen the tall ships when they were here back in June. There must have been a dozen of them, just majestic as they sailed by here. It was like stepping back in time."

I could picture it clearly. Just being in the condo was a different era for me, a step ahead though, not back. It was such a pleasant night that we decided to walk to the restaurant. When

we arrived I was surprised to find Donna's two daughters waiting with small presents in hand, anxious to meet me and help
celebrate my birthday. Both were in their late twenties and dread-
ing hitting thirty. They were talkative, so before long they had
updated Donna on all the happenings of the week. For the next
ten minutes I ceased to exist, but their animated conversation did
give me some insight into the business. Cathy, the older daughter,
was in sales and marketing while Monica worked with her mother
in design. Neither of them seemed to know much about logistics.
Their distribution was contracted out to a warehousing company
in the suburbs. Cathy had been working hard to get their product
line into a major retailer. All of their products were currently sold
online, but Monica had developed a more exclusive product she
called "No Labels Plus" for retailers. Both girls felt it was critical
to capitalize on their success and expand into a different market
segment that would build their brand. The two of them had a
critical meeting with a key retailer they were targeting to finalize
a pending initial order on Monday morning at eleven o'clock. The
problem was that the revised samples for approval were in transit
from overseas and had been pulled for inspection by customs on
Friday night and the two women were adamant that they couldn't
delay the meeting. Budgets were set and a new supplier could easily be bumped. None of them knew what to do, but I did.

   Our company didn't bring much in directly from overseas,
but I'd had a similar problem two years before. While their customs broker told them they would have to wait, I knew better.
One of my best friends worked for a large brokerage firm and
had expedited the clearance and arranged for us to pick up the
shipment directly at the airport. When I told them the story,
they asked if there was any way I could help them. I texted my
friend, Karin, and she replied immediately that if they could
scan, sign, and email her a power of attorney that she would send
over, authorizing her firm to act on their behalf, she would get
right on it at six o'clock Monday morning and try to arrange for

pick-up between eight and nine. She would email the details early on Monday directly to Cathy. Problem probably solved. I was an instant hero, and, if she pulled it off, Karin had gained a new account for her brokerage firm.

With that behind us it pretty much became girls' night out. Lots of wine and lots of chatter followed covering fashion, real estate, movies, and men. Both of the daughters had failing marriages. Donna had long been divorced and I was too busy to even consider a relationship. None of us cared much about cooking but we did love eating. We shared Alaska crab, lobster tails, jumbo shrimps, scallops, Malpeque oysters, smoked trout, and mussels. The mussels were steamed in a white wine sauce with shallots and tomatoes and served in large bowls. The rest came on two huge platters garnished with dill and lemon slices with cocktail sauce on the side. It was an amazing feast that demanded attention, so we took our time. Instead of birthday cake for dessert, we each had a fantastic apple tart, baked to order, served with homemade French vanilla ice cream followed by our standard decaf latte.

Fortunately the girls had driven so we didn't have to walk home. Monica was the designated driver so she had put down her wine glass early. I was so grateful for Donna arranging that fabulous evening, and was really quite shocked when she generously paid the bill.

"Don't worry, you've earned it. If we can crack this retail account on Monday it'll be a major breakthrough for the company and you contributed."

After a fast ride and a quick goodnight to the girls, Donna and I were back upstairs, exhausted. We pretty well went right to bed.

The next morning over breakfast Donna explained the family problem that had brought her into Sam's latest group. I had been wondering, but on the surface nothing was obvious. I knew it had to relate to one or both of the girls since they were her only family in the business. I thought it might have to do with succession issues, but Donna was young enough that it wasn't imminent. I hoped her health was fine. That morning it just poured out of her.

"I've lost control of my business. My girls are growth-crazy and I think maybe I've hit Sam's precious Peter Principle and I'm in over my head. You know the one that states that we all continue to get promoted until we reach our level of incompetence. Maybe my business has outgrown me and I need to slow it down. The girls don't see it that way, but they both work in specialty areas and leave all the other details to me. I can't handle it. I'm being forced into decisions I don't want to make and inevitably I'm going to make a mistake and blow the whole thing."

I doubted that. Donna had a well-established niche with a great reputation and I'd already seen how bright and determined she could be. A little reassurance couldn't hurt.

"We haven't known each other long, but I'm sure that's not the case. You're talking about it so you're not ignoring the problem. You just need a solution. Have you talked to the girls about your feelings?"

"How can I? They're so happy. I mean, I felt the same when I first started. I can't let them down." Her voice was full of anguish.

I realized that Donna was too emotionally invested to think clearly. The solution didn't seem that complicated. Maybe I could help analyze the possibilities.

"Well, you have a few options. Promote one of the girls to take on more of your role. Give both girls more responsibility. Slow down the growth dramatically. Sell the business. Or bring in capable help to round out the team and reduce your workload."

We discussed the pros and cons of each option as we drove back to the inn. By the time we arrived Donna had become so absorbed in the solutions that she was confident she could solve her problem. I wasn't positive which way she would go, but we had certainly exhausted the merits of each possibility. Before leaving Donna had packed a cooler full of the seafood left over from the previous night. We shared some of it with Mike, who was the only other one back at the inn. No one else was due back until the next morning. Mike had spent a full day hiking around the area, which was part of the Bruce Trail–Niagara Escarpment network. He'd met several other hikers and even done some climbing with two new friends who he planned to meet there again the next weekend.

It seemed that the three of us had made the most of our brief time off, so a quiet night was welcome. Mike settled down to watch Sunday night football while Donna and I went up to our rooms before nine o'clock to watch Downton Abbey. There was an afterglow that I sometimes felt after an uplifting new experience. I'd made a good new friend and felt that the friendship would last. The weekend had been short but full. Being busy had taken my mind completely off my decision. When my issues started to creep into my mind I focused on the Crawley family problems, which dwarfed my own. I was asleep five minutes after the show ended, maybe sooner.

CHAPTER FOURTEEN

A New Era of Entrepreneurship

The two prodigals, Jeff and Steve, arrived separately just prior to the three o'clock start but Tim wasn't there for the Monday session. Sam, of course, was right on time.

"Before we get back on track with our family issues, I'd like to expand our conversation from Saturday. There's tons of evidence that entrepreneurs have been a driving force in history. For one thing, most exploration was driven and financed by entrepreneurs. As we expand the reach of globalization it seems to me that we've built the wrong structures to handle it. Globalization fuels competition. It fosters the best and most efficient use of resources. In our fast-moving world business has to be flexible, resilient, and adaptable. Innovation is the most important factor in finding new comparative advantages that keep the economies of individual countries vibrant. These are qualities that are inherent in small entrepreneurial firms, not the large international behemoths that we've created.

"Our business schools have focused on producing executives for large and expanding corporations. In that sense we've been floating a flawed business model. Only in the last few years has entrepreneurship become a new emphasis. If flexibility is critical in this environment, doesn't 'too big to fail' really mean 'too big to succeed,' or maybe just 'too big'? We've abandoned microeconomic theory, disregarding principles such as the Law of Diminishing Returns and economies of scale. The benefits of globalization lie in capitalizing on comparative advantages around the world and translating them into the most efficient system for the provision of goods and services. These huge companies do seize on the obvious comparative advantages. That's why we have large manufacturing plants in China capitalizing on cheap labour and expanding outsourcing of services to India taking advantage of their inexpensive tech capabilities. These glaring advantages are easily identified. However, it's going to take entrepreneurs looking for opportunity and focused on making things happen that dig into the many other less obvious opportunities. Also, it will take entrepreneurs to solve the issues of comparative disadvantages such as non-competitive unskilled workers in developed countries. Transitioning to a true global economy can be painful. These disadvantages are serious threats in many countries because they create structural economic and social problems that can't be exported. Entrepreneurs will see opportunity in these disadvantages and set in motion projects that will alleviate them, maybe even solve them over time. In the simplest terms the right people can and will make bad ideas work in tough circumstances.

"It's not just about the money. Most entrepreneurs stick to their own area. At a time when globalization is running rampant, entrepreneurs often practice localization, finding opportunity in their home area and creating jobs for others where pure economic logic says don't try. This is why I place such a high value on all levels of entrepreneurship. The philosophy is not about making money, it's about making things happen. High-profile success is critical. It provides inspiration and encouragement to huge numbers of people to whom success means a more modest achievement that collectively impacts society. So I encourage you to travel as I did and seek ideas and contacts that allow you to build your business in your backyard. None of us can build in a vacuum, so local success must be immersed in global knowledge. This is a new era of entrepreneurship, where the future of the independent society that we value may depend on entrepreneurs to maintain individualism and resist the trend to build huge monolithic entities that can doom us to job instability and inefficient management, building disproportionate wealth through profits achieved by capitalizing on inequities around the world."

Had Sam forgotten it was Monday? Pretty heavy stuff to lay on us first thing, but as usual it was thought provoking.

"Give some thought on how you need to adjust. We've only got a few days to complete this course development, so back to the joys and challenges of family business. Let's expand some more about team building; we missed compensation last week. How do you feel reward structure impacts your team when family are involved?"

Typical Sam, interject some random higher level manifesto to make you think and then deny you the time to respond until later. I wanted to ask him more about his statement. Most of us are so busy covering our day to day needs we ignore the bigger picture. Sam had a colloquial style that made it easier to relate macro-level problems to day-to-day life. Like most of us he was fascinated with the success of high-profile entrepreneurs. That was made clear, but he always found ways to relate those achievements back to the minor successes of everyday entrepreneurs like us. Baby steps as he called them — the baby steps of millions of entrepreneurs around the world were the key to solving social and economic problems. If you were part of the club, you were part of the solution. I'm sure all four of us were having similar thoughts. After a short group hesitation, Steve spoke up about compensation.

"We talked about nepotism denying opportunity, but that issue relates more to the roles within your team. A worse scenario evolves by giving outsiders on your team roles and responsibility but paying family members more. It comes back to loyalty and entitlement issues. Too often family members who underperform or can't perform are overpaid. Since its human nature to pay ourselves, at least once the business is established, either you underpay yourself or severely overpay other family members who feel they're entitled to the same as you. Either you sacrifice, or more likely the outside employees do because the reward pool is impacted, or even worse the business itself suffers. If the employees feel the pain, you'll lose some good ones. Family can become a non-productive overhead that eats up the profits."

Sam was pacing across the front of the room, appearing a little agitated.

"It's a mistake I've seen repeatedly. Don't think you can hide it. Someone will find out and this kind of reward system becomes destructive. Worse if you've lied about it. This is an issue that undermines leadership, creates mistrust, and reinforces a 'them versus us' mentality. You don't want that attitude in your business. Steve talked about this last week. Fathers are the worst, taking one of two approaches with their sons: either they are destructively tough or they're foolishly lenient. Parenting inside a company mirrors parenting outside a company. I'm not sure about mothers and daughters. What do you think, Donna?"

Having just seen her daughters in action I thought Donna might be too easy on them. Her dilemma about her ability to control them reflected that and Sam knew it. We were both watching her closely as she answered.

"It hasn't been a factor yet, but it could be. I have been too easy on them both in terms of demanding responsibility and rewarding them. I've had to — both are getting divorces and they need the money. The main reason their pay hasn't caused an issue is that we have a very small team. All of our distribution is contracted out."

Sam was still pacing. "You just can't pay relatives based on their needs. No one else would. All your employees have needs. Family needs often lead to multiple payouts to keep things equal, which can stress your business. It comes down to business interest

versus family interest again. In the early stages they're insepar-
able, but once you evolve into an active business with significant employees they have to stay separated. Donna, you may not
believe it's an issue yet, but it is. Remember what Steve just said:
one of the downsides is personal sacrifice. If you're being too easy
on them or overpaying them then you *are* the one paying a price."

That was bang on. Donna was hanging her head like a six year
old whose hand was caught in the cookie jar. Sam didn't even look
up, he just moved on.

"Last week I mentioned how the DuPont family implemented
a parallel reward system so that employees distinctly shared in
the success of the company despite being denied high-level
management positions. It's not perfect, but it has sustained the
company for over 150 years. You have to be innovative in rewarding everyone in the firm just as you do in every other aspect of
your business. Having family on staff just adds one more complication that can't be ignored. The Rothschild family ran a banking
empire across borders in Europe for close to two centuries. Only
family members could become partners, but any general manager who reached forty-five was given a huge severance and set
up in his own smaller bank. Can you imagine how that motivated
the outside employees? Whether its profit sharing, sales bonuses,
percentage of savings, or something else that's brilliant, you need
to customize rewards that motivate your staff and either elimin-
ate or offset alternative family rewards. Whatever you do adopt,
the incentives have to be linked to achievements that ensure the
success of the business. I've seen ridiculous sales bonuses paid
out on low margin sales that effectively bankrupted a company.
Simple systems are the most effective, but make sure they are not
so simple that other consequences penalize your business. Take
the time to think through all the implications."

Donna still looked uncomfortable. I was sure Sam hadn't
meant to embarrass her. Not only was he challenging us all at a
higher level but he was really forcing our hands on the problems

that we'd submitted. He was willing us to find answers, not giving solutions from an outsider.

"Let's move on to a different topic: funding. How does the family dynamic impact funding?"

Jeff spoke up for the first time that day. "The influence has to be positive, especially for startups in areas that aren't high profile. If anything, it's too easy. Family members don't hold you to the same standard. They want to believe you. Any other lender or investor is more demanding. If the entry level of entrepreneurship is as critical as you suggest, there has to be dramatically more startups through financial support from family than there would otherwise be. Plus not all family-funded businesses turn into family-run businesses. There are lots of solo entrepreneurs who get their initial funding from family members. That's a big issue to me."

I still thought Jeff looked familiar. His hair was starting to grow in and it was red. I was sure I'd seen him somewhere before, and recently.

"Family funding is the original crowdfunding," Sam said. "The bigger the family, the bigger the crowd, and the greater the chances to raise funds. Not only are the initial funds contributed, but so are tons of sweat equity to keep costs down. Absolutely we have many more startups because of family trust and support. Even some of the prominent tech startups have benefitted from initial family funding. For the small startup, this key type of financial support gives the entrepreneur the courage to make the leap of faith that leads to a solid business. Of course there are numerous examples of failures that follow, but seldom does the family regret. So family funding is definitely beneficial in the startup phase, but what about later on?"

"I have some personal experience with that" said Steve. "When my dad died the bank almost called our loan. The company was established but our banker viewed my dad as the business. With him gone, the bank insisted on an equity injection to pay down a significant part of the company's loan or they would call the whole thing. I had to raise two hundred thousand dollars in a week. The extended family came through. No one wanted to see my dad's legacy squandered, so they raised the money for me. Within two years I had paid them all back, but I couldn't have survived without them."

Sam was calmer now. "That's the type of story you hear often. When there's a threat family will bail you out when no one else will. Banks can take unfair advantage by tying up excess security just because they can get it. But that's a whole other issue related to personal guarantees. What about when the business is growing beyond the family's ability to supply the necessary funds?"

Jeff had an answer. "It can backfire. If you need to bring a venture capitalist to the table, they tend to be suspicious and reluctant to get involved with family situation. They're totally focused on return and profitability. They don't want any distractions that might compromise the results. Access to capital is a major hurdle in taking the family startup to a growing established business."

Sam was not big on venture capitalists and often referred to them as "vulture" capitalists, so there was a slight hint of sarcasm in his response. "You know my high regard for VCs. They play an important role in accelerating and growing startups that have huge upside, but they're not a serious option for most mainstream small entrepreneurs. Bankers have their commitment to formula banking that can approve losers and reject winners to meet preset lending criteria, rather than using their judgement. That policy is anchored in mediocrity and averaging out. VCs have their parameters and they require rates of return that can violate the entrepreneur who is impatient to develop his company. If the returns are high enough it works out, if not the entrepreneur can lose his soul and end up with nothing. That's why I like bootstrapping — short-term pain for long-term gain. Keep your equity if you can, but it does take longer."

Donna brought up something that I knew was on her mind. "What do you really think of crowdfunding, Sam? It seems to be a growing alternative for small business at a stage when traditionally we're forced to stretch our reliance on friends and family because the banks aren't ready to look at us yet. Is it too good to be true?"

She had mentioned the idea over the weekend. Donna was serious about launching a campaign once the regulations were clarified.

"I'm in favour of anything that increases the funding options for independent business. I just hope this one doesn't become overregulated. Definitely you should consider it for your business, Donna. Your customers are online savvy and they like your product, making them natural investors that can be easily reached. Ideally crowdfunding opens up higher return options for small investors who are willing to take entrepreneurial risk with the hope of high return, at the same time providing much needed capital for companies who shouldn't have to give us as much of the pie as they would to a venture capitalist who would never look at their business in the first place. It should bridge the gap between the family investor and bank funding, even facilitating dealing with the banks if you can combine the two. That could help entrepreneurs preserve equity and leverage results for the original owners and their new investors. I would negotiate with the banks for preapproved loans subject to raising a certain amount of equity through crowdfunding. That would be part of my offering. There's great potential here, but it has to evolve more before it can definitively impact lower profile companies just emerging from their startup phase."

At that Donna smiled, evidently encouraged by the possibilities for funding the same growth that she was not sure she wanted. Entrepreneurs can be fickle, especially about growth.

It was time for Sam to make his daily pronouncements before sending us on our way to the Brewhaha. Our group decision to ignore them hadn't dampened his enthusiasm.

"So I'm going philosophical on you today. First point: 'If, as Marx said, religion is the opiate of the masses, then optimism is the drug of choice for entrepreneurs.' And for a change of pace from that: 'Entrepreneurs believe that they can change the world and right now, the world needs changing.'"

None of us looked up or acknowledged the comments. The little game was extended, Sam wouldn't take the bait.

CHAPTER FIFTEEN

The Brewhaha Hits the Road

Donna and I were discussing how she could structure a crowd-funding offer when Jeff interrupted.

"All of this talk about India and China has got me thinking. Steve says there's a Mandarin about twenty-five kilometres from here. Mike doesn't have anything prepared, so are the two of you up for a Chinese buffet? Steve has his Mercedes this week so he's offered to drive."

That was a serious offer to bond with us so how could we refuse? On the way over in the car we continued talking about Donna's fundraising project. Jeff was really into it.

"Sam was right, Donna. You've got the perfect platform, a customer network that buys online and loves your product. Every sale's an opportunity to attract an investor." I knew there was more than that to discuss.

"Donna, is it all right if I ask how the girls did today? I didn't have the chance to ask you yet, and when you didn't tell me I thought things might have screwed up."

"I didn't tell you because I wasn't sure how I felt about it. Your friend Karin really came through. Cathy and Monica picked up the samples and rushed directly to their appointment. There was no time to inspect the product, so they were both shaking when they had to open the samples right in front of the customer. The factory followed our instructions brilliantly. It turns out we had a windfall; there were store managers from across the country at their head office so the girls were dragged into the middle of a spring product preview to do an impromptu presentation. It went over very well. So well that the initial order is three times what we hoped. We'll be shipping to all their stores instead of just doing a trial at some of their main locations. That's what unnerved me. I've created a monster and I can't slow it down."

Steve laughed out loud. "The old two-headed monster: growth. What was it Sam said the other day? 'The python that sucks out all of your energy?' We're damned without it for sure, damned with it for trying, and it's damned good news for you Donna. Congratulations."

Jeff was ecstatic at the opportunity to tie in our earlier conversation. "Crowdfunding is a great way to deal with growth. It can be used to raise equity from customers who know your products. This whole crowdfunding idea is almost a populist movement, Main Street, not Wall Street."

We were all really excited for her. Donna and I were sitting in the back. She leaned over and whispered.

"The girls wanted me to make sure I thanked you. If they'd been late they wouldn't have had the opportunity to present to the store managers. I guess a lot of them have tried our products online. That shocked the buyers and probably explains why they increased the order. Thanks so much, Mary. You are a problem solver and this solution really paid off. Now how am I going to handle it?"

By that time we'd reached the Mandarin. The men practically jumped out of the car. Typical guys — all they needed was an excuse to celebrate.

When we stepped inside it was busy but not quite full so we didn't have to wait long. The only hesitation came when we were ordering drinks prior to going up to the buffet. I made the mistake of ordering a diet Coke.

"No way," said Steve. "We're celebrating and everyone knows the best drink with Chinese food is beer. We'll have four Heinekens. Sam said go international, so Dutch beer it is."

Not a good move for me, as I rarely drank beer, and then only Corona, but I had no choice on that first one. Before the night was over, Jeff and Steve had three each, Donna two, but I laid claim to the designated driver role early so that one was it for me. Given the fact that we were famished the buffet proved to be a good choice. Since it was a celebration Jeff imposed a strict rule: no business talk. The beer really broke the ice, if there was any left to break. It gave me the chance to ask Jeff where I might have seen him before but he dismissed the possibility.

"I don't think so. I was at university for the last few years. Unless you were there I doubt you've ever seen me."

I knew that I had, but where could it have been?

The beer buddies sat in the back on the way home and were soon yammering away, engaged in one of their ongoing disagreements. Donna stayed silent the entire way. She had too much on her mind. As we were walking toward the main door of the inn Steve made a declaration that dictated our evenings for the rest of the week.

"In honour of Sam and his instruction to get out and understand international markets, Jeff and I have decided that we're going to eat out all week. Indian tomorrow, Mexican, Brazilian, and Italian to follow. Hope you two ladies will join us." We agreed — one week of quiet nights had been enough.

CHAPTER SIXTEEN

External Intelligence

Tuesday morning started with an early phone call from my brother Tom. Could I call Bruce Hutchison, one of our key suppliers? He had tried to reach me several times in the last week. Both brothers had spoken to him but he refused to explain his problem to anyone else. Since he was one of our major suppliers, my brothers were afraid there was some issue on credit that might disrupt delivery and hold them up in the field. Nothing had happened yet, but since I had the best relationship with Bruce they wanted me to make the call and smooth things over. Bruce ran an independent supply house. He was a crusty older fellow who ran a tight ship, which he needed to do to compete with the large plumbing supply houses. I liked him and knew the feeling was mutual. When I called him there was no trouble at all.

"Why couldn't one of those idiot brothers of yours just tell me that you're on a course for a two weeks? I understand that. This can wait until you get back and it has nothing to do with them. Would you be willing to have dinner with an old fellow one night next week? I have a personal problem to discuss with you."

It wouldn't be the first time we'd shared some personal issues. Bruce was the only business connection I had who knew about my frustrations at work. About three years ago he'd caught me in a weak moment in my office. We were negotiating a large contract for supplies for a subdivision for which our company had won the plumbing tender from the builder. Usually this type of work didn't go to a bid process, but because there were over four hundred houses the builder decided to make it a competitive situation. Our bid had been tight. My brothers wanted the job but I had to put the bid together and when we won the contract I had to negotiate with our suppliers and place all of the purchase orders. The only instruction I was given was "Don't screw it up!"

When I met with Bruce I was on edge and was as tough as nails to him, at least I thought so. But when we finished Bruce offered his hand and said "your brothers are lucky to have you, you're firm but fair. Thanks for the business."

I'm not sure why, but I broke into tears. My frustration came pouring out, fortunately on sympathetic ears. A few months later, when Bruce was in a state of shock over his wife's sudden death from a stroke, I had helped him as best I could. He didn't have any children and since my father had died when I was ten, our friendship grew more or less on a parent-child type basis without the mutual obligations. Sometimes we had dinner together at a local Italian bistro. Bruce was my biggest supporter so I had no hesitation in agreeing to meet him.

"Sounds a little ominous. Can we meet Monday night at Gusto Italiano at 6:30? You're not going to propose to me again, are you?"

That had been an ongoing joke between us for the last two years. His answer was short and mildly disconcerting. "Not exactly. See you next Tuesday."

By the time I dealt with all the emails and related issues sent to me that morning, I had missed lunch again and it was 2:45, time to go downstairs.

"Ready for gourmet Indian tonight?" Jeff whispered as I sat down beside him.

"I'm ready now," I said just as Sam got started.

"Today we're going to consider bringing professional help into the family business. It's a tough issue for most entrepreneurs, but seems to be even worse in a family scenario. In any group ownership, it's easy to find dissenters, but the trust inherent in the family business manifests itself in an equally strong mistrust for any outsider, whether employee or advisor, who dares to suggest, change, or imply criticism of a family built institution. Combine that tendency with the reality that most families don't have all the experience or talent required to fully mature a business and you have a dilemma, one that can be a serious limitation. In a perfect world every family unit would include a banker, a lawyer, an accountant, an engineer, and several other professional advisers. Sometimes there's at least one of these within the family who, of course, has everyone's complete trust. Depending on his or her ability this can either be a blessing or a disaster. Family professionals have a captive market, often an undeserved reputation, and a desire to protect both, which makes them either an additional complication or a terrific ally for professional outsiders. Of course, family professionals can be positive team members who are outside the firm and considerably more objective than their relatives on the inside.

"The smaller the company the greater the resistance external advisors are likely to encounter. Mentors are usually parents. The unofficial board meets around the kitchen table on an ad hoc basis. Believe me, I lived this and it happens even when it shouldn't. Education takes a backseat to familial respect. When I was brought into these situations as a consultant, which happened several times, my first action was to establish a monthly meeting that I chaired. The only reason I was accepted as a consultant for this type of business was because of my background in a family company. I could identify with the personal issues and the business issues on their level. It allowed me to penetrate the circle of trust.

"There's an expression about leading a small business that says you must be able to fly high and fly low. You have to be able to relate to the talented and the challenged. That's equally true if you want to be an advisor to family-operated businesses because there usually is a talent gap. If you can understand and operate within the culture you can lead changes that will make the company more successful. Most professionals struggle with this reality, expecting automatic respect for their expertise. I found success first by gaining trust myself and then gradually recommending other professionals with whom I had worked, such as lawyers and accountants, as specific problems arose. Over time this became the new normal and the companies built up their own network of trusted advisors. In all of these situations I acted as a pseudo-controller until I could convince the owners that they needed to bring someone on staff who had the credentials to become the CFO. Once they had a financial officer in house they soon saw the benefits of control.

"All the while I embraced and respected the family structure, usually becoming a de facto board member, even if there was no official board. Patience was critical. As the businesses grew I directed them toward a more formal board, eventually bringing in others to give advice. This approach worked extremely well when the newcomers had solid industry knowledge. Once that was demonstrated the board became an effective advisory group and the business became more professional and more successful. The family council can and will emerge into a board of directors if the business matures and the owners do as well. Otherwise the business will be mired in the mud of self-deception, limiting its potential and making the owners indentured labourers to a family dream that cannot be fully achieved.

"This really is a case where the family entrepreneurs need to be disrupted and pushed off the complacency of their initial achievement. It is a process of revitalization. Sometimes the renewal is postponed and finally happens from within under the leadership of the second generation, like you, Steve, where the next generation has been educated, often in a business school. Trusting outsiders comes easily to this generation, as does the recognition of the progress that can be achieved, facilitated by the right outside advice. These children of the founders often bring regeneration to the business. My approach took a lot of handholding and patience with the first cohort, but it did work reasonably well, if at different rates in every company."

Steve interrupted what had been one of Sam's longer statements to date. "Even with her education, my sister has unbelievable loyalty to my dad and his business practices. Her sense of duty overrides logic. I can only imagine how much worse that must be when the family leaders are still in charge."

"As we've discussed several times, there can be a perverse sense of loyalty," said Sam. "A common mistake for first-time entrepreneurs is holding on to a bad idea too long. It's draining. Entrepreneurs have to be resilient and adaptable. A bad idea that becomes entrenched in the culture of a family company is unwavering, mired in a stubborn, unrelenting commitment that is treason to deny.

"Developing effective advisors can be a nightmare. Promoting outside training is also tough because it's viewed as costly, ineffective, and it takes time away from the business. I try and use my coaching analogy since most people can relate to that. When you're developing your son or daughter as a hockey player or ballerina you may be his or her first coach or teacher, but the time will come when you don't know enough to improve their skills. That's when they move to a new level of instruction, one that's based on training to develop their talent. Eventually, if they have real potential they'll go farther until they get the best professional teachers available. Developing business skills is no different. Family leaders can embrace the idea of making their sons, daughters, sisters, and brothers leaders in their industry. Of course the proof lies in the experiment. If the family member embraces the course and comes back with knowledge and enthusiasm then this approach will be accepted. If they pay lip service and come back with no sense of improvement, the idea will die on the vine and the business will suffer. As I said earlier, these problems often survive the first generation but leave the business in limbo until a more informed generation takes over. As consultants we can only try. Of course, there are well-led family businesses that are perceptive enough to deal with these issues, but they're in the minority. I know that yours will be among them."

Donna took the opportunity to ask a question. "These are all business issues that owners ignore, often for trust issues. What about the personal problems that invade the business space, things like a divorce or drug abuse or monetary needs? One of my best friends was recently divorced and the settlement triggered the sale of the family business to allow the payout. Talk about vitriol and hatred. She didn't want to cause the sale but the settlement offers without it were ridiculously low and she had no choice. At some point all sense of compromise went out the window, replaced by a self-destructive bent on both sides. It was horrible to watch."

Sam was shaking his head. I could tell that he'd experienced similar problems.

"Divorce and drug abuse are destructive, plain and simple. Financial needs like your daughters' can be met through loans that have to be paid back to the company without permanently draining it. Drug use can come with success and it can be a terrible financial and emotional drain. Families inevitably get dragged into these issues, so they become more invasive for their company. These problems are just as serious in any firm, but the damage can be more extensive and damaging for the family concern."

I think all of us were doing some mental calculations regarding what could go wrong in our own situations. After a pregnant pause Sam continued.

"You remember the premise that you may be your business but your business is not you. We'll extend that out farther: the family may make up the core of the business, but the business is not the family. Agreements are still necessary to cover various business scenarios such as buy-sell situations or even divorce.

Insurance and funding options to finance buyouts are still advisable. Emotions run rampant in all of these situations, and agreements put in place in more rational circumstances are invaluable. Unfortunately, they are rarely executed or even discussed within the family unit. No one contemplates a breakdown in trust or a material change in their family. Outside advisors who push for such arrangements are dismissed or ignored. It's only when someone sees a scenario like Donna described that a change of heart can happen, but even then there's the notion of 'this would never happen to us.' Balance is a distant goal in any entrepreneurial business, but in the family company things are so intertwined that personal and business needs are blurred beyond recognition. It is only when structure is imposed that there's any hope that these problems can be handled without irreparable damage."

Maybe that's why my brothers didn't want me to have shares — too many complications. Maybe that's why Donna was so preoccupied with the high rate of growth her daughters were pushing. A sudden change in personal circumstances might throw off the entire plan. Maybe Steve couldn't deal with the situation with his sister because no agreements were in place. Maybe too much personal responsibility without a framework to focus on business issues was why Jeff was avoiding his father's business. Duty, loyalty, trust, and the crushing blow that could come if any of these broke down were something to be feared. Yet we were already committed, embroiled in a trial by fire called the family enterprise, at least everyone but Jeff was. I suppose this was reality-check day. I wondered if people who were considering starting a family-based business and took this course would turn tail and run or if they would structure their company right from the outset. I decided there would be some of each, but for the latter there was one key direction — every family business needs a prenup.

But wasn't that true of any partnership? One of Sam's strongest recommendations was that every startup needed an end game — both a means to an end and a mechanism to execute one. A family-based organization had the standard fundamental businesses issues. Even the personal challenges were typical. However, it seemed that the intensity and the emotions for most problems tended to be on a higher plane, while logical solutions could be blocked by a sense of obligation or duty and misguided loyalty. If an employee had a personal problem you would have empathy, and if that concern caused them to leave the business would experience a short-term setback. If a family partner had personal difficulty, his relatives inevitably became embroiled in the problem. If that relative had to leave it could tear the company apart. When family was the foundation of a business, the damage was far more extensive after it fractured.

All of us seemed distracted by private thoughts. Finally Sam broke the prolonged silence.

"Too many negative thoughts. You can almost feel the air getting heavy in here. The last thing I want these sessions to become is a condemnation of the family business. We're still talking about the most effective startup mechanism that we have, the most reliable source of initial funding, and the best sense of encouragement for doubters to take the plunge. These concerns are just problems that need solving, and effective entrepreneurs will solve them! Our goal is to forewarn and prepare, not to discourage."

I felt the need to comment. "I can't speak for the others, but I suppose what I'm feeling is that my personal anxiety could have been avoided if my brother and I had taken a more upfront approach. I suspect that everyone else feels the same, which means your goal of preparing others just starting into a family-based operation is being covered. Forewarned is forearmed, and I just wish that I had been."

And that did seem to be it. Everyone else was nodding, but no one seemed anxious to go any farther today. Recognizing this, Sam launched into his two Sam bits of the day.

"I think that's enough for this afternoon. For my two theories of the day let's start with one that seems appropriate, given your mood, which goes 'Doubt is the forerunner of indecision, while confidence breeds success.' Here's another idea based on kinship: 'Easy is the twin of lazy, while difficult is the cousin of determination; mediocre is the brother of excuse, but success is the sister of effort.' I do expect you back in a more positive mood tomorrow. Maybe a little Indian food will shock you back into reality."

Now how did he know about that?

CHAPTER SEVENTEEN

Curry and Conversation

We were off in no time, bent on Curry in a Hurry, which was the perfect name for our restaurant choice for the night. Mike was along for the ride — it was to be our treat to him for taking care of us every night. Steve was driving but already looking for a designated driver for the return trip.

"My Indian friends recommend scotch with Indian food and I'm definitely looking forward to one. Anyone interested in driving back?"

I had been a little sluggish that morning so welcomed an excuse not to drink.

"Why not? I kind of enjoyed driving your Mercedes."

"My friends always push vodka on me when I'm in India." Donna said.

What followed was a five minute debate on the pros and cons of what alcohol to have with an Indian meal. They both agreed that beer wasn't a good option. Finally Jeff interrupted with a radical change of topic that caught all of our attention.

"I think I've got Sam figured out. I'm fairly sure I know what these end-of-sessions sound bites are about. Our mentor has gone public. Every one of these statements of his are well under a hundred and forty characters. Our boy has moved into social media. Sam has to be on Twitter!"

All of us but Steve, who was driving, and Mike, who probably knew, grabbed for our phones.

Jeff upped the ante: "The first one to find him gets a free drink on the rest of us."

"He's not tweeting under Sam Macleod," said Donna.

"No one's tweeting under Online Studies," said Jeff

I was doing a search under "entrepreneur" when I found him and shrieked out loud. "Here he is tweeting away under @smallbizpreneur. There's the one about doubt that he just gave us. It went out yesterday. That's got to be him!"

There they all were. Mixed in with a whole range of retweets of news items, related to business in general and entrepreneurship in particular, were all of the same platitudes that Sam had been throwing at us. Our Sam was cultivating social media and using us as a testing ground.

Steve was laughing as he drove along. "How many followers does he have? How many tweets has he made? I can't believe that Sam's out there in social media with everyone else."

Jeff was laughing as well. "He has over two thousand followers and he's put out over three thousand tweets. He's been doing this for a while."

Donna was chuckling as well. "Does it really surprise you that much? You knew about this, didn't you Mike?"

There was no denying it. Mike was close to Sam. "Yes I knew, but no one else does except his wife Robin and his publisher, who encouraged him to do it. I'm surprised you didn't notice it before. He's been doing it for over six months and he works at it religiously. Tim doesn't even know. Sam's stubborn though. He refused to do it under his name."

The discovery was perfectly timed. It lifted all of our spirits. The rest of the trip consisted of an animated conversation focused on jokes about Sam and his newfound platform. We were proud that he had jumped in with both feet. None of us were surprised that he had a following even without using his name or his contacts through Tim and Online Studies.

Curry in a Hurry was packed so we had to wait at the bar. We were still yammering away about Sam being on Twitter when the guy sitting beside Jeff interrupted.

"I heard you talking about @smallbizpreneur. I follow him on Twitter. He gives some great advice."

That was the final straw. All five of us couldn't contain the laughter. The fellow thought we were completely off the wall. Fortunately our table was ready but he was shaking his head in confusion as we walked away.

Dinner was highlighted by Steve and Donna introducing the rest of us to a real Indian dinner based on their travels; all kinds of dishes that I would never had tried on my own. Most of it was south Indian, so vegetarian with a strong influence of chili peppers, black mustard seed, turmeric, and cumin. Fortunately the restaurant had their servers do a taste test first to establish our tolerance for spicy food and they served yoghurt in between dishes to cool down your mouth and throat. If we'd listened to the two travellers we would have burned out our taste buds to their great hilarity. Mike made the mistake of accepting their advice on the first dish served and was gulping down the yoghurt while the two experts shrilled with laughter. Jeff and I were sympathetic but soon joined in, although we had learned a lesson in the process and remained cautious for the rest of the meal. The breads were fresh and delicious: naan and roti to dip in a wide range of sauces and dishes. We chose a couple of northern recipes such as tandoori chicken, which I had eaten before, but most of the others were new to me.

It was a great night and a definite bonding experience. Steve's suggestion of our own mini international meal tour was a great success. As I drove back to the inn it was hard to concentrate. Everyone was babbling away with no thought of business or family problems. The main topic was the Mexican, Brazilian, and Italian nights ahead for the rest of the week. It was a nice feeling to be part of a like-minded group that loved being in an independent business. As Sam said, "a true entrepreneur loves the process more than the project." As I drove back deep in my own thoughts, oblivious to what the others were saying, I understood exactly what he meant.

CHAPTER EIGHTEEN

The Lecture on Localization

Wednesday; four more sessions to resolve my dilemma and the time was passing fast. This whole exercise reminded me of going to camp for two weeks when I was ten: making new friends, learning new things, having new experiences, only to come to an abrupt end, which was now on the horizon. Sam was the camp leader, Mike was our counsellor, and the rest of us were the campers, a mixed group for which the camp was the common bond.

I spent a listless morning, frittering time away in a half-hearted attempt to answer my emails. I microwaved my leftover food from the previous night but it didn't taste quite as good, sitting in my room, alone, watching the news of the day. I felt confused about our family business. I had a touch more understanding of my brothers, but I was not at all sure that staying in the fold was the right answer. Maybe if my parents were alive I could have used them as a sounding board. If they were I might not feel the same sense of obligation. I called the office to speak to Ted. I thought hearing his voice might strengthen my resolve one way or the other, but he was out in the field as usual. He was very good at what he did and we both knew that I had his back as my parents would have expected. But was that compromise really the best for either of us?

That was my state of mind when I wandered into the conference room two minutes late. I was the last one to arrive but I realized right away that Steve and Jeff were toying with Sam. Steve was speaking.

"Have you found anyone interesting to follow on Twitter lately, Jeff?"

"Funny you should ask," said Jeff. "I think there's somebody out there tweeting out Sam's sound bites. I thought it might be you."

"No, not me," said Steve. "Maybe it's one of the girls." He looked right at me.

Donna and I both shook our heads at the same time. Donna answered for us both. "No, not us, but both of us checked it out after Jeff mentioned it last night. Whoever it is, he's a pale copy of Sam, not insightful at all, and his statements are just platitudes. I'm sure he stole them all from someone."

Sam was standing at the front of the room, hands on hips, glaring at Mike, who was grinning from ear to ear.

"Don't blame me, Sam; you wanted to keep this to yourself. These guys just figured it out all on their own. Maybe you should have kept your tweets to yourself."

Sam turned back to us.

"Are they really that bad? I'm finding this social media thing tough but my book publicist says I have to build up a new platform and that's the place to do it."

We respected him too much to keep playing him along. Besides, we wanted to help him. Jeff was more into Twitter and LinkedIn than the rest of us.

"Nothing wrong with your content Sam, but keeping it a secret blows your biggest asset. Tie into your network. Your contemporaries aren't online, but people like us who have taken your seminars are, and all of us will promote you. How did you ever build up the following that you have without using any of us to jumpstart your followers?"

"I just worked at it for a few hours a day. I learned to use hashtags, and I retweeted the best news stories on small businesses that I could find, and finally I added in a few platitudes like everyone else. Then I made sure I tweeted in the morning first thing, in the afternoon between four and six, and at night after ten o'clock. That's still my formula. Before I knew it, I was over two thousand followers and counting. I've been stalled lately, so I could use your help."

For the next few minutes the teacher became the student. All of us made suggestions, including revising his schedule to send out tweets automatically and making commitments to take turns retweeting his content, giving him more exposure through our networks. He was also trying to start up a blog, so that discussion took another ten minutes. By that point Sam had heard enough and he wanted to get started on the day's session.

"At this rate you're going to be here for an extra week. We ended yesterday on a downer, with too much emphasis on problems and not enough on the solutions, plain and simple. First, here's a short overview. A family business is still one of the most common and best foundations to launch a business. There is no better option for most of us for a combination of physical, emotional, and financial support. That's the premise upon which we built this series. Some of the largest, most successful business in the world started as family-based entities and some have stayed that way as huge operations. Without sounding like a broken record, what we're trying to accomplish here is to set a definition of the issues that can come up that are compounded by the makeup of a family business. We want to protect the interests of both the business and the family. They're not the same but neither are they mutually exclusive. In today's dynamic world these concerns come up sooner for those businesses that are growing at a fast rate. What we want is for more of these businesses to mature and survive into future generations. That's more difficult today than ever before."

At this point Jeff interrupted. "Is that even realistic in today's global economy? Don't you think that the life expectancy of any business is shrinking due to competition and speed of change? Maybe building a dynasty isn't in the cards anymore."

I noticed that Jeff's hair was really growing in and was just long enough to show a distinct shade of red. I was positive I'd seen Jeff before. Sam's answer distracted me from figuring out when and where.

"Of course the dynamics of the world we live in are key factors for any business, but every problem is an opportunity. This new era offers many positives for entrepreneurs as long as they stay flexible and adaptable. There is one side of a family structure that does disturb me in this environment. I've lived through the decline of an industry. Even worse, we had a vibrant business that was growing within an industry that was shifting to Asia. If we hadn't gone overseas to assess the competition we would have held on too long and the business would have gone beyond its expiry date with no chance to survive. Recognizing this early and selling the business made a huge difference in my career. What I did notice at the time was that the owners of many family-based companies refused to accept what was happening. One of my best friends, who followed our example and convinced his brothers to sell their second generation business, had a severe bout of depression because he felt that he had betrayed his father. Others continued to operate well beyond logic. The very things that support the start of the family business doomed them. Encouragement and sacrifice can lead to perverse bootstrapping, bent on preserving the tradition and image of the family resulting in serious damage to wealth and to the future of the family members. That's exactly what happened to several people that I knew well. It's sad to watch and so counterproductive. That same effort put into a new venture would have rejuvenated opportunities for many. Entrepreneurs are the most adaptable players in the economy, but emotions have to be taken out of the equation so that the determination, which defines an entrepreneur, doesn't become misdirected. Survival requires change, but obligation and duty to salvage the status quo can be destructive when its day has passed. That day will always come, perhaps sooner than expected, but the need to renew a company has long been a fact of life. No business can move into a third or fourth generation without reinventing itself along the way several times over. But in today's global economy it's actually become a first generation problem, and an ongoing one at that, one more component that's driving a new era of entrepreneurship. Survival at all costs is entrepreneurial; survival without change is a recipe for disaster. It's no different than hanging on to any bad idea, there comes a time when you have to let go and move on, directing your energy into an area with a better chance of success. It's easier said than done when family is involved."

Sam stopped for a drink of water, giving us a chance to speak out. Donna went first.

"You're making me wonder if it would be better to invest my profits differently, provide for my retirement and invest in my daughters' education, or maybe start something different for them rather than relying on my business for everyone's future. You seem to be suggesting that success is a fleeting event and it could change on us quickly."

"You already know that. You were in business in 2008, you were small and growing so you sailed through it without slowing down, but your growth would have been greater and you certainly saw the impact on your competition at the retail level. All of you have to provide for retirement — the idea that future profits will be there when you need them is foolish. As far as your daughters are concerned, that's a very subjective question. Your business is just starting to mature. Their best option and yours right now is making this venture work. Just be prepared to change gears as things change."

"Don't you think it depends on the nature of the business?" I asked. "In our online course you talked about China-proofing your business. It made me confident at the time. Our plumbing business is here and now, not so subject to imports."

"That's just one source of competition," said Sam. "What if someone revolutionizes the industry with new materials requiring different expertise or a major investment in equipment or if they develop robotic plumbers for home use? What if all the home builders vertically integrate and take plumbing in-house? You'll have to adjust, and fast! Finding a career that is less susceptible to foreign competition makes sense, but that's not a lifetime guarantee of security."

I heard Steve humming "La Bamba" so I knew his mind was already on dinner. Oblivious to that, Sam finally started his topic of the day.

"I want to expand my thoughts about localization versus globalization that I touched on the other day. Entrepreneurship really is a local phenomenon, and family business in particular is a bastion of the neighbourhood and the community. The culture of loyalty and duty that permeates a family company is far reaching and extends from their private lives out into the public. My friend Keith is a great example. Like me, Keith has changed industries several times in his career, moving from manufacturing, to retail, to real estate, but all within the same small community about sixty-five kilometres west of here. He's been an ongoing source of job creation for his home town for the past forty years. I've often asked him why he didn't move into other geographic areas where there was more upside but he had no interest. He's a great example of the adaptability and resilience that characterize being an entrepreneur. He loves the process of building a startup, but he likes staying put and investing in his own backyard.

"Big business looks for opportunity around the world. Entrepreneurs generally invest in their home and find opportunities that others ignore or just don't see. Entrepreneurs make things happen where they want. The right people can take a bad or questionable idea and make it succeed. The wrong people can take the best idea and destroy all the potential. In the face of global competition, which is intent on restructuring our world to allocate resources and activities more efficiently based on comparative advantages, we desperately need leaders who can make borderline ideas work. Leaders who can look at pockets of structural unemployment and see an opportunity that is viable for them. That kind of leadership isn't forthcoming from the behemoths that we have created. A real entrepreneur would never use the defence of 'too big to fail' as a rationale for government to protect them from the vagaries of the market.

"To some degree our business schools have created a flawed model, graduating executives as opposed to entrepreneurs, pointing our best minds into the creation of a culture of control and a business bureaucracy that moves slowly, making it vulnerable to huge mistakes. A hundred years ago the landscape was full of small communities developed as company towns. History tells you that businesses took advantage of a captive labour market, which was probably true, but these same companies were also prime sources of local philanthropy. They sponsored local sports teams, encouraged and rewarded students who went on to university, built libraries and sports facilities, and they provided stable jobs for many. The character of the community and the social life revolved around these companies and the programs and resources they provided to the community. If you study the history of Bell Labs, which may well have been the largest single source of innovation in the twentieth century, many of their most brilliant minds grew up in these small communities. One reason is that within those towns there was interaction from the head of the company down to the floor worker. The original idea of flying high and flying low was a natural phenomenon in that setting. Floor workers could talk to the owner and sons of floor workers could aspire to become an owner while working summer jobs that gave them exposure to how a business worked. Admittedly the whole world was more localized. Most businesses had all their customers within a five hundred kilometre radius. The business world could not have been more different from today's environment of fast-paced global economy.

"So why even mention it? Many of these businesses were family owned and operated. Often they evolved into large operations, some of them international. They are not the right model for today, but the sentiment behind them to invest and donate locally will be increasingly important as we struggle to compete internationally. This trend has been underway for some time. For the past forty years the West has sustained its leadership in the world economy through research and development. Initially that kept our factories in North America occupied making new products. Investment in innovation gave the West the advantage of first in to the market with a wide range of products and for a while we continued to stay ahead by doing things better and different. Then, as greed will do, new products were transferred offshore by exporting new technology to gain cost advantages. More recently large companies have kept control through distribution to the consumer market primarily through branding. Most of the large producers in the East have no concept of how to market here, but just as Japan gained the knowhow, others are following suit, not only into our markets but into their own domestic markets, which are gaining in buying power. Welcome to the reality of a world economy in transition dominated by large corporations pursuing low costs around the world like locusts eating off the backs of cheap labour and ill-informed suppliers.

"If we have the twin goals of maximizing production efficiency around the world and achieving full employment worldwide then our best bet is to have governments concentrate on the social issues that suppress entrepreneurship around the world such as culture, education, gender, funding, and so on. Given the freedom and ability to do so, entrepreneurs will pursue comparative advantage as opportunity and attack structural issues as a different type of opportunity on their home turf. Governments need to understand their role. Big business needs to as well, although they will be busy maximizing profits by contracting out to more efficient entrepreneurial firms and by pursuing growth through acquisition. Entrepreneurs will continue to be the agents of change. Disruption within the bastions of bureaucracy, big business and big government will be essential to approach anything remotely close to optimal operations. The key to reducing the cost of government is disruption. The growing discrepancy in wealth between the haves and the have-nots will deepen unless more of us have the chance to pursue opportunities as entrepreneurs. Otherwise we are headed back to early- and pre-industrial revolution times where upward mobility was limited, the middle class was relatively small, and the discrepancy in wealth between the rich and the poor was extreme. We are in a state of a grand transition, or at least we can make it grand, or we could slip back into a state of listless domination by wealthy interests.

"So back on topic, where do family entrepreneurs fit in this analysis? One more point from my own experience, when we sold our manufacturing business, which was indeed the love of my business life, we did have another option. We could have packed up all our equipment, taken our expertise and some key supervisors, and started a plant overseas. Without a doubt this would have been profitable, but it ignores the human element. Instead we stayed here and invested locally, creating more jobs and finding other opportunities. I know people who did move off-shore and on a business basis they have flourished. If you believe that you live to work perhaps that's the right path. It's a little like selling your soul to the devil. Unrestrained greed leads to bubbles and ultimately to huge social problems. Without local investors primed with local interest we will have major social disruptions around the world, and this is not the form of disruption that we need. Just look at Detroit: recently bankrupt with enormous numbers of defaults on housing, resulting in low real estate prices and a very high rate of unemployment. Entrepreneurs are already looking to start businesses jumpstarted by the low cost of real estate and labour. There are better investments elsewhere in the world but these investors are looking close to home. That's how we solve structural problems from a business approach. From a government approach these people need real education and an improved ecosystem leading to job opportunities. Entrepreneurs that are the most prone to this type of local investment are family business owners."

This was quite a change from the previous sessions where we had been encouraged to exchange ideas and raise doubts. Sam was very wound up, and I for one didn't want to interrupt. Apparently neither did anyone else.

"Sorry to run off at the mouth. I just feel passionate about the future and how we should approach it. Economists generally preach the benefits of globalism but don't talk enough of the fractures that occur along the way to a perfect economic world where all resources are used to the maximum benefit in the most efficient way. What may be desirable from an economic point of view may not be feasible from a political or social point of view. We need an economic mechanism to effect the transition in a way that minimizes the social pain and leads politicians to a solution. In my mind the only possibility is through unleashing entrepreneurs of all stripes and all levels across the world. Look at Japan, a society where chauvinism ran rampant until very recently when the business leadership has had to make a choice between encouraging women in business or promoting immigration to support an aging population. The decision was to preserve the homogeneity of the population at the expense of long-established social values related to male dominance. Women are gaining opportunity while immigration policy remains tight. That's just one of the many changes on the horizon, but it has unleashed a wealth of entrepreneurial talent from one source that was previously suppressed.

"From a business point of view, a similar thing has happened here in the West, well founded on both economic reality and the impact of technology. Women are starting as many businesses as men and often they are intentionally small and flexible with family members involved. Many of these companies are grounded in the connection of social media, where networking and creative marketing are skills at which women excel. This development reflects an economic answer to a social problem. For a long time women were being set back by maternity leave. Mothers out of the work force for several years were having trouble getting back in and were often pushed down to inferior rolls. Every problem has a solution, and entrepreneurs are problem solvers. These new careers are local jobs so local they are often done from home initially but then evolve into more. Donna is a good example — initially a mompreneur, now the founder of a family business right downtown where she can walk to her office. How great is that?"

Donna was beaming but none of us wanted to break the spell.

"The trend for women to start businesses that suit their lifestyle has helped deal with a significant developing social and economic problem. The idea that lifestyle entrepreneurs don't count is ludicrous. Everyone needs to find their own balance, and these jobs solve problems and make things happen. Big business is completely onside, all too willing to take advantage of flexible, adaptable entrepreneurs in any form by contracting out. These big, lumbering giants need flexibility, and this is one way they can attain it. Government is joining in as well but tends to create contract positions more than contracting out. That may change. All of these are examples of more to come as our society adapts to the reality of global competition and the need for the creation of flexible jobs. From an individual point of view the complexity and uncertainty of this transitional period all point to the value of the ability to create and manage your own career. I know you've heard it before and you can count on hearing it again. The theme will be prominent in my book and of course, on my Twitter account. Which reminds, me it's just past five and I need to share a couple of new tweets with you. First we have 'Entrepreneurship takes many forms. The common bonds are the personal issues and the fundamental business challenges.' And secondly, to cheer you up, 'Entrepreneurship isn't a spectator sport. Teamwork is critical. The bench is thin and all the coaches must play.' Based on your off-key humming, Steve, I suppose you're all off for a taste of Mexico tonight. Better take Mike along since he's crossed over to the dark side. Have fun."

What a session. I entered it flat and lifeless. Now I felt restored, refreshed, and galvanised. I was no more certain of what I should do, but fairly confident that my options were good no matter what. The others were equally upbeat as we headed out to the parking lot to resume our mini world tour. Sometimes the reality of being on your own, in a way that only entrepreneurs can appreciate, is a lonely, even scary existence. You either thrive on the independence or you wilt and retreat into employment, which is fine for most people. Sam had reminded us that an important key to independence and control over one's destiny rested with your ability to create and manage your career. If there is no such thing as job stability, is it that risky to strike out on your own? If opportunity is disappearing in the face of wealth disparity between the wealthy and a shrinking middle class, why not take a shot at creating your own upside? Maybe circumstances are going to create a new generation of entrepreneurs with or without leadership. It was a nice feeling to be on the creative side of the equation where risk was managed and opportunity encouraged.

CHAPTER NINETEEN

Mexican Asada

Mike was the designated driver that night. I had a craving for an ice-cold Corona, perfect for our Mexican theme. The trip to the restaurant was a repeat of the previous night, full of upbeat conversation focusing on Sam and his Twitter experience. Steve and Jeff were busy congratulating themselves on flushing Sam out. Donna was talking to Mike about her daughters.

I was still damned sure that I had met Jeff before. His outburst of laughter was strangely familiar. Where could that have been? Just as we arrived at the restaurant it came to me. His name wasn't Jeff Michaels and he had no intention of going into his father's business. What was he up to in Sam's class? I decided to wait until later to expose him. What would be the best way? maybe something that mimicked what Jeff had just done to Sam? I would enjoy that and I was delighted to have gained an advantage, which I decided to keep for a while. The rest of our little crowd were oblivious to my little intrigue as we walked into the Mexican grill.

The place was packed with locals so we had to wait at the bar for the second night in a row. Fake Jeff and Steve were talking to a group of local college kids and before we knew it both were sucking on limes and knocking back margaritas plus paying for the whole group. Guys just don't seem able to grow up. Donna and I were about half way through our Coronas. Naturally the kids loved it and I had to admit it was fun kibitzing with a bunch of twenty year olds, but Mike was getting a little concerned. Finally after the second round we got our table, leaving the college group behind at the bar happy to have a third round at Steve's expense. At dinner Mike directed our overgrown male zealots into coffee for the rest of the night. This didn't stop Steve from lecturing us all on the critical importance of the blue agave plant in producing first-class tequila. It was entertaining, but neither Donna nor I had much interest. Once the coffee arrived they were soon debating the pros and cons of Mexican versus Cuban versus Brazilian. Jeff trumped them all by introducing Turkish coffee into the debate. They were acting like a pair of immature macho types, sharing a drink at the end of the work day, bragging about things they knew something, but far from everything, about. Donna and I thought it was hilarious. The restaurant was an *asada*, or grill, so Steve ordered a whole range of grilled chicken, beef, pork, shrimp, and lamb to be sliced up so we could all have fajitas. Before long there were several sizzling pans on the table containing the meats plus fried onions and peppers. Guacamole, sour cream, salsa, and warm soft tortillas arrived and we were all engaged in hand to hand combat filling our tortillas and our faces. You can tell something about people by how they eat fajitas. Mike, Donna, and I were fairly tidy, putting less on each tortilla. Jeff filled his more but took great care to fold in all the corners so that nothing leaked out. Steve's tortillas were loaded and the salsa was dripping on his chin, but he was enjoying things the most. He needed the break; of all the family issues I believed his was taking the greatest toll. He was clearly tormented about redirecting his father's company and his differences with his sister magnified his guilt. Of course I knew now that Jeff didn't actually have a problem with his father.

Donna was getting more relaxed as the week went on. Mike was telling her about Sam and Twitter. "He's really the same about everything — relentless, totally obsessive-compulsive. For a while there he was averaging thirty new followers a day and treating his computer like a video game. Then he switched over to LinkedIn and averaged six new connections a day until he built that up. In contrast he's totally digitally challenged, won't text, and won't even give me his cell phone number because his cell is for his convenience, not for anyone else's."

Both Donna and I were giggling at the thought of Sam hammering out tweets and following a host of young bloggers trying to figure out social media. "How does he really feel about all the success in tech? There are so many twenty-somethings that have been huge successes. Does he respect that?"

There was no hesitation. "Oh Sam thinks they're great examples, a key part of the culture of success he believes in, but he does worry that tech gets all the attention and most of the capital while entrepreneurs in other fields get ignored. You've heard the party line — all levels and types of entrepreneurs contribute. Sam's connected with quite a few techies on LinkedIn, more than I would have thought. They respect him, and vice versa. He's been invited to do some teaching and offer a seminar program at a prominent business school, but that's not for publication. He's enjoying his retirement, if you can call it that. I can hardly keep up with him."

"Do you really think it bothered him that we found out he was on Twitter?"

"No way," said Mike. "He meant it when he asked what took you guys so long. He's been looking for all of you to start following him since you signed up for this series. He doesn't publicize it but it gives him a kick when his would-be entrepreneurs find him, especially some of the older ones. His publisher's been pushing him to open a website of his own and publish his Twitter address and his LinkedIn profile. It's good for the book business, but Sam is stubborn. He likes the challenge of building this up from the bottom. No doubt he'll tie it all together before the book comes out."

By this time, the fajitas were all gone, so Frick and Frack were listening, in the process remembering how embarrassed Sam had been. Mike was having none of it.

"Get serious you two. Sam's only embarrassment was that it took you so long to figure it out. He follows both of you and neither of you has even noticed. I made him promise not to retweet you or comment on any of your posts and that has been driving him crazy. Same thing on LinkedIn — I wouldn't allow him to make connection requests to any of you. Donna was the only one who found him on her own."

Another surprise, she could have told me. She read my mind and looked at me right away.

"Sorry Mary, you know Sam, he made me promise. I found him by accident when a friend retweeted him and I recognized one of his quotes from the first set of seminars. At first I thought it was someone else quoting him, but when I followed him, he followed right back and sent me a direct message. It's been fun watching him on social media, most guys his age can't be bothered, but he wants to be part of it."

That was the last word before we left the restaurant. We had just settled the bill so it was time to leave. No one was really surprised that Sam was taming social media. The drive back was more subdued, either from the long day or the heavy meal taking its toll.

CHAPTER TWENTY

Succession: Is the Family Business Model in Danger?

I spent part of the next morning researching the real Jeff Michaels. He was hardly the type to be pressured into joining his father's business. Actually he was a very interesting guy, far beyond the persona of his alter ego, who had been cozying up to Steve all week. I had seen him speak at an entrepreneurial conference at the university — he was a tech millionaire at twenty-three. At the time he had long, curly red hair and looked more like Raggedy Andy than a tech genius. What was he doing here in a development program for a series of seminars on family entrepreneurship? Did Sam know? Or maybe Mike or Tim? After Donna's revelation about being connected with Sam on Twitter maybe they all knew. Regardless, I was armed and ready when I walked into the meeting.

I didn't even give Sam a chance to get started before jumping into my own charade.

"Sam, I hope that you don't mind, but I have a special guest to introduce. This entrepreneur has conducted one of the most dramatic startups in memory in this area, while keeping the focus on staying here and building jobs and opportunity here instead of exporting them abroad."

Fake Jeff might have looked uncomfortable at this point, but I was determined to keep him off balance.

"In that sense this experience reinforces your belief that entrepreneurship is a local phenomenon. He has received international recognition for these achievements and for a strong commitment to promoting entrepreneurs."

By this point Donna and Steve were listening along with everyone else. Fake Jeff was hanging his head with a sense of inevitability. I was enjoying myself.

"Unfortunately our guest has developed a penchant for deception that belies his sterling reputation."

The jig was up and "Jeff" knew it. "All right, Mary, that's enough."

But I was determined to finish what I'd started. "Please Jeff, let me introduce someone you know very well, a legend in his own mind, tech entrepreneur Peter Charo, who is unlikely to be considering going into his father's business."

Steve and Donna were looking around for someone to come in the room. The rest of them, Sam, Mike, and Tim, were laughing out loud. Jeff/Peter was just pissed. There was no other way to describe his reaction. Sam wisely took control.

"All right, Peter. There's no sense losing your cool. We owe them an explanation and I'll give it."

Donna and Steve were still confused.

"Peter is one of my protégés, my first tech entrepreneur. His father sent him to me for a one-on-one consultation. That's why none of you realized the connection. Peter has a legitimate reason for being here, but I'll leave that up to him to tell you. As far as any deceit is concerned, he wanted to sit in with a diverse group of business owners without attracting attention. It was my idea to give him a different name and appearance. Tell me, wouldn't it have affected the whole program if you'd known who Peter is? That wouldn't have worked for any of you."

Steve and Donna were in shock, having had no idea. If looks could kill, Peter would have been my assassin. As for me, I was all smiles, pleased with my detective work. Witnessing the consternation within the group Sam moved to smooth things over.

"Look, the dynamic hasn't changed. I'm sure Peter will give you more details but you'll have to discuss this on your world tour tonight because we have one of the most critical family issues to discuss today — succession.

"North America is approaching a crisis regarding business succession, one that doesn't get enough attention. Collectively, small business creates jobs and a surprisingly high percentage of private sector jobs exist in companies employing a hundred or less. One outgrowth of the baby boom is that hundreds of thousands of small business owners are approaching retirement. Their dilemma is succession or sale. In most cases the principal asset and source of retirement funds is the business. Are we going to have a glut of businesses for sale in the very near future?

"As for succession, it has long been an ongoing challenge for any family business, but today we have a generation gap that's widening, increasing the resistance for the next generation to become involved in a family business, never mind take it over. On the opposite side, the life expectancy of any business is much shorter than in the past. The idea of a business even surviving for two generations has become questionable without the suggestion of staying in the hands of the same family entity for longer. So there's two reasons why the problem of succession may become irrelevant but if it does become a realistic goal, I've seen the process botched by some very bright people.

"One of my best friends transferred control to his son to attract him into the business only to have the son get a divorce without any prenuptial agreement. There had been no need at the time of the marriage because the son wasn't in the business. That business had to be sold and my friend, who had accepted preferred shares and a great consulting contract in the process of transferring control to his son, was a big loser. I've seen sudden deaths where a surviving wife, with no understanding of the business, insisted on vesting control with a son with no ability to run the business who squandered the assets for personal use. There are always entitlement issues. The commitment to succession varies in importance in different countries with some such as the U.S. putting a higher value on keeping ownership in the family than others, like Canada, where the business is more of a tool to generate wealth, not to maintain a goal. Wealth itself can lead to myriad possibilities or it can be squandered, but so can an inherited business. Wealth is more flexible. That's why every business needs an exit strategy and transferring the business to the next generation is just one option.

"With baby boomers hitting retirement age in record numbers the disposal of a business may be disappointing. With so many businesses up for sale, many of them won't find a buyer. For those that do, low interest rates impact income and wealth preservation strategies. Frankly, most family businesses are very dependent on their older generation, making them vulnerable to disability or death. Insurance is a huge factor in succession planning and wealth preservation. The problem is that the majority of family businesses have no contingency plan other than insurance. Of the large number of first-generation businesses facing transition issues, the majority have annual revenues between two and five million dollars. Collectively they do employ large numbers. In an era where job stability is weak and wealth differentials are rising these companies offer a fantastic platform for those who can inherit. If only they were prepared. There are many niche sectors such as trucking, farming, the building trades, or construction itself where meaningful opportunities are being ignored or resisted by a reluctant next generation. Denial of duty and obligation has kept them out of the business, which means many of these businesses will be sold or mismanaged. There are great opportunities just to continue and there are others to grow by acquiring like-sized competitors.

"This quandary seriously impacts retirement planning for the first generation since a forced sale due to no continuity can mean a big reduction in asset yield well below expectations. As this situation evolves it emphasizes the importance of building up assets outside your business. You simply can't count on your business to provide cash for retirement when you need it. Sometimes an employee earn-out can salvage the situation and transfer the opportunity away from the second generation to the experienced upper and middle management of the company who have supported the founders. This gives the founder continuity of pride, both in the company and the new owners who he or she has trained, and it usually results in a higher sales price. It's more or less a win-win scenario.

"Occasionally, I've seen the opposite of being unprepared — what I call the Harold Ballard syndrome. Ballard was a well-known owner of sport franchises who put a succession plan in place prematurely in his fifties. By the time he died at over eighty tax laws had changed, the interest of his children had changed, and the plan was ill-timed and off base. Decisions and financial structures put in place too early just don't anticipate how people evolve, tax structures shift, and, most obvious, business circumstances transform. The only constant in planning is change, so plans must be flexible enough to deal with varying circumstances. Like any form of planning the process should produce a framework for adjustment, only finalizing things once they happen. In estate planning, the word 'estate' is an adjective. If the structure is too rigid in the face of change it can be a disaster. Never forget that in planning any element of your future the one thing we can be sure of is change. Whatever plans for succession are put in place, they have to be revisited and revised regularly. Just look at poor Prince Charles; he'll be sixty-five next week and he hasn't even become the head of the family business."

Sam was in high gear and for the moment the Peter Charo controversy was forgotten.

"This is another area where a board including outsiders can be a huge advantage, particularly if there are competing family members wanting to take the lead. It is not in the best interest of the business to follow the example of the royals and pass control to the oldest child. Businesses have to be run on ability and initiative, not bloodlines — at least not strictly on bloodlines. A legitimate board with a reasonable outside interest is far more likely to make the selection of who should assume the leadership role based on merit than a family council burdened by a sense of duty and entitlement.

"Founders like to pick their own successor and if possible mentor them, but times have changed. Wealth preservation trumps business control. Like any idea we won't relinquish, holding on to a business too long can be damaging. Every business owner has to have a business strategy. Painful as it might seem, selling the business on a timely basis when you are least vulnerable may be the best option for both the business and the family, but especially for the family. We've repeatedly discussed the premise that the ability to create and control your career may be the most important skill you can learn and we've also stressed that you have to have an end game. I personally believe that fostering a culture of success created by understanding the philosophy of entrepreneurship combined with an inheritance of flexible wealth outdoes leaving a business behind that is on a path to decline or failure. It takes a heavy-handed reality check to accept this and it is definitely a change in philosophy from past generations, but it's prudent. More than ever you cannot create your children in your own image. Henry Ford learned that difficult lesson with his son Edsel, although he didn't accept it until it was too late. In today's environment that lesson is critical.

"There are a host of issues that impact generational differences from work ethic to the environment. Many second or third generations simply don't want the lifestyle that their parents adopted. They remember the parental absences and the lack of vacations and they don't want to inflict that on the next generation. There are negative implications to growing up in an entrepreneurial family. Even so I've found that the philosophy often survives when the business is passed elsewhere. It's better to provide the education and the resources to allow for an entrepreneurial career with better opportunity, which is exactly what Peter's father did for him. It seems like we've abandoned the concept of succession in terms of mandated continuity, but not really. How many times have we talked about what's good for the business versus what's good for the family? The balance has shifted, but there are still many examples of both intergenerational success and succession. Sustaining the business is still a goal for most founders. Legacy issues may encourage you to transfer leadership to a family member, but the real legacy is a business that survives even without a family member. Selling is still a form of succession whereby the interests of the family finally become divorced from those of the business, a happy day for many spouses, at least initially, until they suffer the consequences of withdrawal.

"If you do pass on a business to one child when one or more others have positions with the company it can be destructive. Appointing a mediator can avoid a rash of problems, from open warfare to a rush to leave the company out of frustration. It's tough to assume control when both your mentor and the core of your team have gone. The mediator's role can be as simple as acting as a neutral chairman for critical negotiations, keeping things moving, and tempering the emotions that are prevalent. I've filled that role several times. It's not easy and it forced me to try and interpret a late friend's feelings at a time when I had lost them — not easy for a friend but worse for family. If a family successor is the choice it needs to be announced well before the transition, at least two or three years, to make sure that person wants the role and to work out all the challenges involved. There are definitely many businesses and families for which this is the right decision, just not as many as there used to be."

Finally a comment from Steve: "I wish that my dad had made the succession clear before he died. I do think he trusted me to take the company into a different economy and to make the changes required. My sister needed to hear it from him."

"Sam, what am I going to do?" Donna asked. "My youngest daughter is the most capable, but my older daughter is the one that wants it. How am I going to reconcile that?"

Sam didn't hesitate. "Better get your advisory board in place and have a mediator in mind, some outside board member who both daughters respect. Whatever you do, don't bury your head in the sand. If you recognize this tendency now it's probably here to stay, but who knows, one of them could get married and move to Brazil."

That produced a laugh from everyone, including Donna.

"Whatever you decide, put a mechanism in place, not a rigid solution that presupposes conditions. Things change. So on that repetitive note of warning it's time for my tweets of the day. How about this one first: 'Entrepreneurs love the process more than the project, the challenge more than the reward, and the solution above all.' Such wisdom in a hundred and forty characters or less. Secondly, a more basic sentiment that I penned with the help of my grandson: 'Failure sucks! Learn from it if you must. Avoid it if you can.' That one's for all my associates that insist you have to fail in order to succeed. Managed risk beats reckless risk hands down. I know many entrepreneurs and the successful ones are adept at assessing risk. Failure is not in their vocabulary and it shouldn't be in yours. So enjoy the night, and Peter, don't be too hard on Mary. I'm sure she thought we were up to something more than we were."

CHAPTER TWENTY-ONE

Churrasco Fiasco

We almost called off the tour that night. Mike wasn't going and the rest of us were divided along gender lines on whether I was off base in calling Peter out. Finally I offered to be the designated driver again and we did set out. The real reason we went was that none of us had ever been out for *churrasco*, Brazilian-style grill. When Sam described his first trip to Brazil he raved about the lunches, including all you could eat chicken, beef, pork, and lamb plus a beer for a total of four dollars topped off by a huge plate of hearts of palm, which he loved. He described the waiters walking continuously around the room with large chunks of each type of meat on a sword-like skewer and slicing off chunks whenever you asked. We wanted that experience.

One convenience about staying at the Speyside Inn was the seclusion in close proximity to the city. Steve had located an authentic Brazilian churrascaria in the west end, well within reach. It was about a forty-minute drive, which we made almost in silence. A few minutes before we arrived I thought that I'd better speak up.

"Okay Peter, why did you sit in with us? Was it for the entertainment value? I resent opening up to you about my problems when you were pretending to be someone else. What was the point?"

"I suppose I owe you all an explanation, but I do have a family problem with my business, just a different one, and it does involve my dad. You see, when I was just getting started, after about six months I was out of money. I had stopped going to class and my dad found out. At first he was furious but when he understood what I was doing, he decided to fund us. He carried the ball right up until the first venture capitalist committed for five million. After that money was never an issue. So even though I'm this big self-made success I still had to rely on my parents to get started. That pretty much destroys the image, don't you think? That's part of the reason I asked Sam to protect my identity. The other reason is that I just wanted a normal experience again. I haven't been able to go out like this since the breakthrough three years ago. The red hair's a giveaway. People either know it's me or they think I'm the snowboarder Shaun White. Either way there's no privacy. I've enjoyed our little tour these last few days. It was worth shaving my head."

Steve was smiling. "So all this time we've been dining out with a multi-millionaire. Who would've thought. I guess tonight's on you. But what's your family problem? I'm sure you paid your dad back."

Peter shook his head.

"He doesn't want the money back, and I gave him shares so he's doing well. It's worse than that; he wants me to take my sister and brother into the business. That would destroy my team. I mean, we've got a cool group of tech buddies that hang out 24/7 doing cool things. I mean, this has got to be the best time of my life. It doesn't get better than this, and adding family out of convenience is the kind of thing that could destroy the culture we've created. My dad doesn't get it and that's more of a problem because he just won't accept no for an answer. He's the determined entrepreneur type that Sam keeps talking about. The two of us aren't speaking so I have to resolve this mess and soon. My mother calls me and cries on the phone. What am I supposed to do? Same old shit — what's good for the family isn't good for the business."

That pretty well broke the ice and Peter was back in our good books. His problem was as at least as bad as the rest of ours. He belonged again. By the time we got to the restaurant things were back to normal. When he confirmed he was buying, things were totally kosher.

We had definitely found a taste of Brazil, but there was little drinking that night; for whatever reason we were all more serious. Sam's message about globalism and reaching out to entrepreneurs in other countries was resonating. Our little world tour was a joke, but it was a solid reminder of the reality that we needed to be proactive. Peter's platform was picking up subscribers all around the world and he was preoccupied with picking up advertisers in very different markets. It turned out that he had some involvement in picking up marketing agencies around the world and admitted he had no idea what he was doing. He had to rely on a domestic agency with international affiliates to solve the problem, but it had given him some chance to travel. I was the only one who hadn't travelled out of the country. That was one of the things that I was going to change.

The food was fantastic, pretty much the way Sam had described it, and we all ate well. Neither Peter nor I had any of the lamb and that proved to be fortunate for us. Both Donna and Steve and the iron-cast stomachs that they bragged about from their trips to India suffered some kind of food poisoning. I had to pull the car over several times on the way back to the inn while they took turns throwing up. Since the lamb was the only thing that they had eaten that Peter and I didn't, it had to be the lamb.

So that was the Churrasco Fiasco — not a big argument between Peter and me but a heavyweight encounter with food poisoning for our travelling partners. By the time we got back they were feeling a little better. Mike was still up and gave them both some clear broth before bed that seemed to settle things down.

Peter and I made our peace. We sat up talking for about two hours with Mike over coffee. Peter's experiences were unreal. We can't always choose our opportunities, but the best set of circumstances came together for him — he was that rare individual who combined the ability of the innovator with the drive of the entrepreneur. He was one of the superstars that could do it all and had. I was jealous, but he was the antithesis of self-centred, encouraging me to strike out. Peter swore he saw the fight and the drive in me that I would need, all I needed was the right opportunity. By the end of our long and animated conversation I had made a new friend. I would never have struck that note with Jeff.

CHAPTER TWENTY-TWO

Dispute Resolution

Peter and I had talked deep into the night, so for the first time since we arrived at the inn I slept in. When I finally did get up there were surprisingly few emails to deal with. Everyone at the office must have been winding down for the weekend, though it was surprising since it was November and house builders were pushing us to get their houses fully plumbed. I guess I wasn't the only lazy one; Steve and Donna were recovering from their substandard lamb and stayed in bed until Mike brought them up Jell-O and clear soup for lunch. At least all of us showed up on time, right at three o'clock, somewhat worse for wear but ready to move ahead. There was no time to talk to the others before Sam got underway.

"Just a few personal comments before we wrap up the session. I've mentioned that as a parent you eventually learn that you can't plan your children's lives. In a way, at least from the family side, that's what succession issues attempt to do. That may be an age-old intergenerational problem, but it's magnified today by change. For example, people are having children later in life, so the average age difference between generations is increasing. Combine this fact with the reality that social, economic, and technology factors are evolving much faster than in the past, add in demographics, and you'll find that the issues that impact career choice between generations now are more like those that used to exist between three generations or even more in the past. Many vocations that attract young people today didn't even exist thirty years ago, while other long-established careers are disappearing. These new jobs just don't derive from tech; look at all the opportunities related to elder care. We can thank entrepreneurs for creating a whole range of new options with many more on the horizon. The chances of following a career path set by your parents have diminished greatly, and if you are entrepreneurial they're even less. The best opportunities are in new industries or professions. These undeniable trends, combined with the decreasing longevity of corporations or businesses of any kind, make succession issues much less significant. The end game of building a family empire is a fading dream replaced by the goal of a high-priced sale to an industry behemoth — sad but true.

"In the past many people defined the family business quite strictly as one for which control will pass to the second generation. The issue of succession was the defining element. However, this trend to a shorter shelf life is not the end of the family business. Every startup requires funding, support, and teamwork, and families will continue to be a prime source of all three. The emphasis needs to shift from a focus on the longer-term family business to the original incubator — the family startup. In the past maybe 30 percent of family firms survived into the second generation and far less than 10 percent reached the third. Those percentages have declined, but startup activity through a family network has not, and I predict it will actually increase due to factors like job instability and structural unemployment."

I found this disappointing and wanted to pursue it farther.

"Sam, don't you think the family goals can still be accomplished? It just won't take as long. I mean, if wealth creation is the principal goal of building a family empire, developing a business fast and furious can do that in ten years, not fifty. Also, the same talent can do it again or invest as an informed venture capitalist based on experience and create even more wealth. It seems to me that the opportunity is still there, just in a different form."

Steve interjected a touch of sarcasm. "It's a good thing we're going to create all this wealth because one of the jobs that didn't exist thirty years ago was financial planner and every second person I meet now seems to be one."

That comment got a laugh from everyone, including Sam. "Good point, Steve. You look a little pasty today so I'm glad there's some life in you. Of course, you're right, Mary. We're talking about the timing and form of wealth succession versus business succession. Early sale of a business diffuses important issues such as the suitability and capability of the next generation to run the business and the destructive elements that can result from competing heirs, plus it's much easier to divide and customize more liquid assets. The opportunity and ability to do this relies on entrepreneurship, which is why managing your own career is the path to upward mobility and the solution to wealth disparity, at least on an individual basis.

"Before we move on, you've probably missed my anecdotes, so here are two from my own family history that illustrate the frustration that can result from succession planning. My grandfather was a veterinarian who graduated from the Ontario Veterinary College in 1905. While he established a thriving vet practice he was also an entrepreneur with foresight. Seeing that the development of the car was going to impact his large animal practice, he continued as a vet but he also became the only car dealer in the community, selling Model A Fords. With four daughters he developed a succession plan that included my mother enrolling in the commerce program at the University of Toronto. My mother was just sixteen and she was the only female in the class. That proved to be too much pressure, so she transferred into an arts program. But what really undermined his succession plan were circumstances beyond his control: first the Depression and then his premature death in 1933. As a result, entrepreneurship in our family was put on a hold for an entire generation.

"The second story involves my in-laws, who had a modern successful tanning operation in Czechoslovakia. The largest shoe manufacturer in the word for many years was Bata footwear, which originated as a Czech company. Family lore has it that the founder of Bata used to come to the family tannery to pick up leather in a wheelbarrow. That business lasted three generations until the combination of the Second World War and the communist takeover of Czechoslovakia destroyed it. That was a setback, but the entrepreneurial spirit revived here in Canada in the following generation. The best laid plans are never guaranteed. As in every other area we have to depend on resilience and adaptability to sustain a business or to rebound from a serious setback like a war, depression or premature death. But more than ever in this fast-paced global economy we have to focus on an end plan and one that is consistent with a shorter time horizon. Every business has its due date that no entrepreneur wants to go beyond. Duty aside, it's not easy to sell your baby, and that is one of the biggest challenges some entrepreneurs have to face. For others affecting a sale is second nature and always part of the plan. We all have to shift in that direction. Businesses can and will continue to survive succession, but in all probability the percentage will decrease substantially."

That suggestion was thought-provoking for all of us. Peter certainly had the opportunity to sell his business for big bucks. Donna had obvious succession issues that might be irrelevant if the businesses didn't outlive her, and it probably wouldn't. Steve had to be a seller based on his problems with his sister. As for me, I had no control or significant input; I was the stereotypical duty-bound dependent relative. That had to change. Before anyone could comment Sam switched the subject.

"Enough about succession. Let's move on to another key topic: dispute resolution, something all of you need to learn more about. Friction in any business is unavoidable, from the classic office politics scenario of a large corporation to the ongoing father and son debate over the direction of the family business. Friction between generations often focuses on work ethic and value judge-ments. Today's millennial generation places a high value on social contact and social media, which interrupts the work day. Their par-ental cohort sees this need as immature, counterproductive, costly, and inefficient. What they don't choose to see is that the millennial generation is very productive because of their knowledge and use of technology. To put it into perspective, my grandparents would have thought of the five day, thirty-five-hour work week as wasteful. Values change and productivity takes different avenues. Friction within generations of a family business often stems from birth order and childhood experiences. Jealousies exist and carry over into adulthood and business. Worse, they get suppressed and fester because of duty and passive acceptance of long-established traits. I have had at least two friends who left successful family businesses because of toxic relationships with siblings that might have been resolved at some point but were suppressed for too long, ending in a major blow up and irreconcilable differences. The bottom line is that if you choose to accept the problem for a long time and finally explode, you become the focus because your behaviour changed and the norm that you established has been broken. Breaking any pattern of consistent behaviour, no matter how damaging it has been, shifts the blame to the one who changes. Too often disputes are delegated out to professionals; lawyers accountants, or consult-ants who more often or not treat the symptoms without addressing the underlying issues. There has to be a better way."

At that point there was a sharp knock at the door. Sam continued to speak as he walked toward the back of the room to open the door.

"I had hoped to be farther along in this discussion, however Mary had her surprise guest yesterday and I have some of my own today." He opened the door to a small crowd, some of whom were very familiar, and said, "Please come in."

To the shocked looks on the faces of everyone in the room in marched my brothers Ted and Tom, Donna's daughters Cathy and Monica, and five others I didn't know. Sam soon rectified that by introducing everyone. Even Mike and Tim, who was there for the first time all week, seemed completely surprised.

"All of you know some of these people very well but I'm probably the only one who knows them all. We've had an evening meeting this week. You see, I didn't think that any of you were really confronting your demons, so we're going to do that today. None of you are going home tomorrow without progress, and that starts with open discussion. So to help with that we have Cathy and Monica Simmonds, who are Donna's daughters; Tom and Ted O'Brien, who are Mary's brothers; Jeffrey, Lauren, and Jacob Charo, who are Peter's father, sister, and brother, respectively; and finally Paula Jacobi and Dave Cameron, who are Steve's sister and brother-in-law. I haven't told them anything, just asked a few questions and gained some knowledge from their perspective. One thing I do know is that delaying the discussion only deepens the problem. I have a long history as a fixer, so who wants to go first?"

There was a hostile, overwhelming feeling dominating the room. I was shaking in trepidation but trying hard not to show it. A conflict I had been postponing was staring me in the face. The visitors were no different. Confusion and concern were plastered all over their expressions. Based on our long conversation last night I was really surprised that Peter's father was there. Their conflict sounded bitter and irresolvable. Sam was taking an unbelievable risk. I could only hope that it didn't end in anger. There was a fine line between resolution and ruin. It was clear that the various other sides of the equation were no more eager to start.

Finally Peter, who had less to lose because his relationships were already strained, spoke out, but first he went over and hugged his father. That was the first encouraging sign. I tried to listen carefully but my mind was racing, desperate to figure out what to say. One of Sam's last comments before everyone arrived stuck in my mind: if I exploded my brothers wouldn't understand. I had to take the emotion out of my remarks and make a logical case, just as Peter was starting to do.

"Dad, you know my position. Why did you bring them here today? Are you trying to shame me? No offence Lauren or Jake, but I just can't introduce my siblings into a culture that has evolved through sweat equity and friendships that have deepened through accomplishment. Resentment will result, my team will decay, and the business will suffer. The whole idea will suck me into a vortex of protectionism and oversensitivity with me spending time defending my siblings or my friends instead of optimizing my business. I won't do it."

The words were not quite as encouraging as the hug. Jeffrey Charo followed suit with a very conventional pitch that just didn't resonate in the same way.

"Peter, you owe it to me. You know there's no future for them in my business, I have to wind it down. I helped you gain tremendous success and now I want you to do the same for Jake and Lauren. It's your duty."

Peter wasn't buying it. "Dad, my business may be over by the time Jake is ready. Companies simply don't last that long, not anymore. I will never forget the opportunities your great business has given us all, but I won't jeopardize my company to replace it."

The battle lines were emerging rather quickly and the discomfort in the room was increasing, at least on my part. Sam knew he had to diffuse the conflict so he asked a question.

"Jeffrey, the other night we were talking about your first business. Can you just summarize what you told me? I think it might help."

"Well, it was a little like how you started. My friends and I had gone to Mexico right after university. We fell in love with the Mexican leather sandals, they were called *huaraches*. None of us had ever seen them before. We started importing a few to sell, then started our own retail outlet and sold the sandals and other types of clothing and gifts, all from Mexico. We did it for two years, four good buddies, and then we went our separate ways, but the experience sold me on having my own business and I made enough money to start one. It was nothing like what Peter's done; we worked like dogs, but I've never had so much fun doing business in my life. By the way, Peter, it was Sam's idea to bring Lauren and Jake today, not mine."

Sam was still smiling but Peter look stunned.

"You've never told me that story before. All I remember is you working long hours and travelling away from us. I don't think I've ever heard you use the words fun and business in the same sentence. You just said your start was nothing like mine, but you're wrong — it's exactly like mine! Only my sandals are software and my market has taken off. My friends are an integral part of my success. Dad, please understand that."

Before the senior Charo could answer Sam turned to Lauren and Jake.

"Do either of you have anything to add?"

Lauren could hardly wait. "I haven't told you this yet Dad, but after I finish my MBA I'm going to New York to study fashion. I have no interest in Peter's business. The only reason I came today was to meet Donna Simmonds and discuss her business."

Her father looked appalled, then the younger brother, Jake, added to his consternation. "Dad, I'm a freshman. I just want to make my way through the next four years and see what doors are open to me. I like what Peter has done, but more for how he's done it than what he actually did. You let him find his way; I need to find mine."

Mr. Charo was speechless, having just received a strong dose of reality. As Sam says, you can't plan your children's future. Sensing momentum, Sam didn't give him time to react.

"That's great and more than enough to digest for today, everything's out in the open. Let's leave it there. Who wants to go next? How about you start, Donna?"

I think all of us were a bit relieved that Peter had scored some points without spilling any blood. Whatever the reason, the discussion started to flow more naturally beginning with Donna.

"Strange as it is, this conversation is overdue. Unlike Peter's dilemma with his father, this has nothing to do with you being in the business but everything to do with the way we're going about it. I personally can't sustain the growth rate you two have cultivated. I never could say no to either of you, but when you're totally aligned it feels like being run over by a steam roller every morning and arriving home at night like a limp puppet. I am really concerned that our business is outgrowing me. I feel like I've already reached my level of incompetence. We either have to slow down or build a much stronger support team in the operations side of the company. Whatever we decide, I've learned a lesson. If any one of us has concerns like this we have to share openly and stop worrying about feelings, duty, or emotion. As difficult as it may seem, our business rapport cannot revolve around our personal relationship."

Cathy and Monica both looked relieved. After exchanging glances Monica spoke for both of them.

"Thank God. We both thought you were sick. Until Sam called last week we thought you were away somewhere for treatment and weren't telling us. You've been troubled and listless for the past few months. We know you too well not to have noticed. When we saw you and Mary last weekend we felt better, but we knew something was wrong. Mom, these are solvable problems that need serious discussion. We know that you take on too much without complaining, which means this is all about overload, not incompetence. You're not running our home as a single mom anymore; this is a business that needs business solutions. Let's start next week when you're back in the office. I already have some ideas. I'm sure that Cathy does too."

Donna was clearly relieved. Wouldn't you think that communication would be easier within a close-knit group of family managers? Of course, I knew better. But mothers and daughters almost always got along well; brothers and sisters were much less predictable. This conclave was moving along far better than I had expected but I was still hesitant and determined to go last. Steve made that easy by launching into a description of his frustrations as he stared intently at his sister.

"Dad would have approved of this approach to resolve differences. He was the first to call a spade a spade and the last to withhold his feelings. Of course he ran the show without any challenge to his authority. I'm glad you that you came Paula. You know it's not disloyal to Dad to make changes. Dave and I have discussed it quite a bit."

That drew an immediate reaction from Paula, who gave Dave a stunned look reflecting a feeling of betrayal. At least that's what I was feeling for her.

"No, don't look at him like that; he hasn't been deceitful. It's pretty normal for the two people in daily operations to discuss the business. Frankly I wish he was disloyal to you, we might have a better dialogue."

Dave was in danger of becoming the target, trapped between the two of them so he tried to cut the tension.

"You two have to talk. I've been listening to both sides and you're putting me in an impossible position. Neither of you is completely right but I can't reason with either of you."

Paula was shifting from side to side in her chair. She seemed uncomfortable discussing private matters in a forum surrounded by strangers. Sam interceded to try and put her at ease.

"Tell me about your dad, Paula. How do you think he would be operating the company today?"

It was immediately clear that Paula had a reverence for her father that was the heart of her differences with Steve.

"Dad was very old school. He loved creating product, so fabrication was the part of the business he preferred. He wanted to preserve the connections with the old country and the traditions of artisan stonework that were generations old within our family. That was the heart and soul of his business and it's what he taught us, not all this trading and distribution of Indian stones. He would have closed down rather than abandon his roots."

Dave squirmed around in his chair but stayed silent. Steve interrupted. "I won't keep going on like this; we can either sell the business, or we can diversify into two distinct divisions, allowing me to pursue opportunities that give me scope to develop while Dave focuses on the fabrication. Or I can just walk away. That's where I am right now."

That was enough for Dave to re-engage. "There'll be no walking away. If these other people can sit down and face their problems we can do the same. Paula, I didn't know your dad well but I do know that he ran this business for over forty years and he didn't run it in a vacuum. He made changes or he wouldn't have lasted. I want you to open your mind and let Steve and I come up with some proposals for diversification and the three of us will sit down and evaluate them objectively. Your dad can't be at that table so he no longer has a vote."

That seemed a little harsh to me, but maybe Paula needed a jolt. Reluctantly, she nodded her head in agreement.

Then everyone in the room turned to me. I needn't have worried; I had built alliances around that room while my brothers were on foreign soil. Donna jumped in before I could speak.

"Ted and Tom, I feel that I know you. Mary is constantly talking about your business and how well you have done. I just want to forewarn you, if you don't give Mary shares representative of her contribution to your company, I am going to hire her away and give her shares in my business. I feel you should know that."

Next was my new best friend Peter. "Just to be clear, if my sister Lauren, who I know is capable, had the interest, the aptitude, and dedication to my business that Mary has shown for yours, she would be a shareholder and on my board of directors. I haven't known Mary long, but I do know that she's a crackerjack and won't be pushed around. I learned that the hard way." He gave me a sideways smile at that last remark.

"To me it sounds like she's been mothering you for a long time," Steve added. "We all take our mothers for granted, but they need to be recognized as much as the rest of us."

All these affirmations instilled me with the confidence to address my brothers. "It's simple really. I love the business and the opportunity. I love that you leave me alone to run my part. My effort matches yours. Both of you should know that by now, but you don't actively recognize it. If you were me, would you stay without an ownership position?"

Ted was more uncomfortable than Paula had been. He could face angry contractors in the field and stare them down, but he wasn't used to a powerful group of entrepreneurs driving an issue so close to home. Based on his being there and the reaction on his face, I had to believe that Sam had found a way to soften Ted's position. I have no idea how he did it.

"Mary, I guess we've been taking you for granted. I know you take care of us and do a lot of things we don't even know about. I'm willing to consider the share issue. I'll review it with Tommy and we'll have a proposal for you next week."

I was speechless. That was it? That's all it took? All I needed was an outside advocate and they caved? Five years of frustration and they were going to give me what I wanted because they finally believed they might lose me. This was crazy! I had a hard time controlling my anger. On top of that they acted like a pair of patsies in front of my friends; that was sure to impress. Was Donna serious? I took a deep breath and counted to ten. At that point Sam elected to call it a day.

"Mike's arranged for pizza and beer. I think I'm going to stick around tonight. Thanks to everyone for coming. This is the first time I've tried an intervention of this magnitude. Like every intervention nothing was resolved here and now, but nothing remains hidden. Let's move down to the lounge area and relax together."

Then as fast as it started the dispute resolution was over. Everything was in the open. Nothing had been resolved yet. At least we were spared Sam's latest tweets. Had this been done on an individual basis there would have been wailing and gnashing of teeth. Blood might well have been spilled. Relationships would have suffered permanent damage. Yet everything here seemed civil. Everyone did stay for the pizza. The two key ingredients were open dialogue and third-party participation. Together the tension was diffused. Now what? Would all of these meetings take place next week or would everything revert to the norm of suppressed feelings and pent up frustration? Only time would tell.

CHAPTER TWENTY-THREE

Italian Innovation

The world tour came to an abrupt end. That night we were supposed to go out for an elegant Italian meal featuring a wide range of antipasto, multiple pasta choices, and a complete range of veal dishes that I had been contemplating all day. Well at least the theme stayed Italian, but it was pretty basic: a choice among meat lovers, vegetarian, or the original margherita pizzas plus a good choice of salads, washed down with ice cold beer. Somehow peasant food suited the in-the-pit style of discussion that had dominated the afternoon. Everyone was famished or nervous or both so Mike brought out the food right away. After the first beer the conversation became more intense and animated, but not confrontational. Sam was getting accolades from virtually everyone, but as usual he remained modest.

"Let's just call today a good start. No problems have been resolved but every problem is an opportunity so now all of you can assess what you're facing and arrive at solutions, whatever those might be. Silence is deadly and I've been sensing near-mortal wounds all week. Prevention ranks well ahead of cure so maybe we achieved the first stage of recovery today."

My brothers were captivated by Sam and spent most of the time listening to him, mesmerized by his anecdotes. He was telling them the difference between Italian innovation and American mass production.

"When I was in the leather industry I visited a large cut and sew plant in Argentina. The company specialized in upholstery leather. The Argentines would cut the hides to the patterns provided by the customer, sew the pieces together, and ship them to the manufacturer who would insert the filling and stretch the leather over the frames to complete the finished product. Their two biggest markets were Italy and the U.S. The Italians have long been known for their styling and quality and their products have generally sold for a premium and still do. During the plant tour I asked the owner what the principal difference was in working with the Italians and the Americans. His answer was revealing. He said that the Americans will fight hard for the price per square foot but the Italians will take the same frame as the Americans and design patterns that look much better. But the real difference is that the patterns supplied by the Americans will take 125 square feet of leather while the patterns supplied by the Italians look much more stylish and use only 100 square feet of leather. That is effective innovation combining style with cost savings and it shows that there is more than one way to solve a problem and more than one way to lower the cost. Necessity is the mother of invention, and that's why cost saving is an element of Italian styling."

I hadn't seen my brothers this awestruck since they'd met Wayne Gretzky at a book signing about ten years before. I'm sure they didn't remember that I had tried to get them to take Sam's entrepreneur seminar online. Regardless, I would make sure that they both got signed copies of Sam's book when it came out. They pretty well stayed away from me, either ashamed or embarrassed. When the two of them left (they were the first to go) I could tell they were contrite and I was pretty sure they were sincere about following through on their offer. Ted's last words whispered quietly in my ear suggested a touch of pride in his little sister.

"You've had quite an impact on some impressive people. It looks like I *have* been underestimating you."

That was it; a major concession for him. Praise did not flow easily across the lips of the O'Brien men. After they left, I spent most of the time talking to Tim and Mike. Neither of them had known about the intervention but they we're excited to have it all on video. Tim was sure it would make great promotional material, provided he could get releases from everyone to use it. That might not be so easy.

There were some animated conversations going on but I stayed out of them. Mr. Charo was not going down without a fight, but the united front of his three intelligent offspring was wearing him down. We all should have such problems. At least he was smiling. Donna and her two girls were huddled in a corner in what looked like a serious business discussion. There was no sign of acrimony there, just an obvious sense of relief. Paula, who might have absorbed the biggest setback of the day, was being consoled by both her husband and her brother. In business two partners ganging up on one to make a decision was the norm, but you didn't see them kowtowing afterwards. In families feelings mattered. My assessment was that Paula could handle both of them, so I was interested to see how their business evolved.

Sam stepped up beside me while we took in the scene in front of us. Quietly he summed up his view of the day and added some personal advice for me.

"Families make for an interesting dynamic; every one of them is different. That was a bit of a gamble for me today, but I think it might work out all right. Just one word of advice for you my dear, don't sell yourself short. The world is moving in your direction, bringing opportunity with it. Select carefully."

Without offering any opinion or clarification of his statement, Sam went on his way. I didn't see him eat a bite or drink any beer. Somehow I had the feeling that he had stayed specifically to influence my brothers. His first love was promoting entrepreneurship, but I don't think that they were the target market. I was.

CHAPTER TWENTY-FOUR

It's a Wrap

Saturday morning — the last session. The cars were loaded and we would be on our way by noon. We all showed up early. Two weeks was a huge commitment for anyone running a business but we all belonged to the club, Sam's little army of Everyday Entrepreneurs, and it was one we wanted to promote and encourage. Developing a culture of success and a belief in entrepreneurship were values that we embraced and that Sam fostered. The spillover effect of confronting our own issues was an added attraction. It was time to get back to work. Sam moved right into the windup.

"The family platform for starting and building a business is under siege. Traditional goals like building a family empire and consolidating wealth for generations to come are finding new avenues, reducing the role of the family platform to a source of startups, which it has always been. The family unit still provides a unique ecosystem for encouragement and support that remains one of the most important mechanisms to promote startups. It may be declining in significance to some degree in the West as crowdfunding offers an alternative source of funds while universities, colleges, and businesses provide innovative alternatives for incubators and accelerators. But around the world the family network remains a critical platform for aspiring entrepreneurs to get started. Suppression due to culture, funding, gender bias, lack of education, and many other social issues continues to limit the effective use of entrepreneurial talent around the world. Family is the institution that best fights against these social limitations. Women are starting businesses in virtually every country, never more than right here in North America. Family support for this exploding source of talent is critical. Husbands are supporting wives. Parents are supporting daughters. Families have always been the key supporter of education, and educated children have provided the path to upward mobility for entire families, often through a business opportunity. We must never underestimate the drive and initiative that comes from the chance to lift one's family out of poverty and into prosperity.

"Breaking down any of these social barriers effectively shifts the entrepreneurial curve farther to the right as more individuals can put their entrepreneurial talent to work. We can move it even farther right with specific education on entrepreneurship. Without a doubt nature is a factor in becoming an entrepreneur. Those on the far right of the entrepreneurial curve combine an innate ability for innovation with a natural instinct to drive for success and an uncontrollable urge to challenge the status quo. They are the ultimate disruptors and the major practitioners of creative destruction. But they are also critically motivating examples of what can be accomplished. The very tough slugging that destroys limitations and changes the status quo for us all comes from the collective action of a growing class of entrepreneurs around the world in every economy at various stages of economic evolution. This is a powerful club and you belong to it. Entrepreneurship can be taught! Entrepreneurship must be taught! Entrepreneurship is being taught!

"Social media is a wonderful way to spread the message. You may not love my tweets but Twitter is a great source of news and information. LinkedIn offers an international network to connect, promote, and learn. All of the existing social media networks, plus those to come, by definition are agents for social change. In a world where globalism focuses on the most efficient distribution of resources and means of production, entrepreneurship is the mechanism that will find these efficiencies. Big business and big government will capitalize on them and mask them to some degree but the real source will come from entrepreneurs.

"We've put the family entrepreneur under some intense scrutiny these past two weeks but no one has made a case for a better alternative. The family business owner remains on the leading edge of entrepreneurship. He is seldom the tech genius like Peter, but may I remind you that Peter grew up in an entrepreneurial culture that influenced him. Don't confuse the introductory level with the optimal level. The key to longevity for family success may not rest in the family business but it often starts there. Maybe this is a better model. Is it better to confine the talent of the next generation to an existing business entity or is it better to provide that talent with every opportunity and the direction to do something bigger and better? In an era where change is explosive and longevity is disappearing, this is surely a better way to go.

"Our business schools do have to change and they are changing. Entrepreneurship, hardly mentioned as a word fifty years ago, never mind a concept or a philosophy, is front and centre at every business school. Our business model has been flawed. It has embraced size to the detriment of economies of scale and the undeniable guideline of the law of diminishing returns. Now in the face of real globalization adaptability, resilience and disruption are the essential tools for growth and improvement. These are the tools and strengths of an entrepreneur."

Sam was in rare form, pretty much on a soapbox but also preaching to the choir. I suppose the video being recorded by Mike could reach a much broader audience. As for me, I felt safe in my options and quite happy to reinforce a philosophy that was rapidly becoming my own. I suppose this is how missionaries convert, by showing a better path to the future. I was just happy to have more than one path available to me.

"At the beginning of this process I reminded you that in the term 'family entrepreneur' the word 'family' is an adjective. An adjective modifies the noun to which it applies. In other words, it alters or transforms the nature of the noun but the noun itself is a defined term. In this case the adjective might imply a variety of things about the entrepreneurship involved. To some it suggests a small operation. To others it suggests a complicated structure. It might conjure up a nurturing environment or a sense of duty. You might visualize stability while others might see instability. Some would envision limitations. Others would welcome opportunity. The family firm certainly has its own culture. Not one homogeneous set of values but a unique value system for each and every entity. Is this so different from any other startup? Duty, trust, and stability: are these not the cornerstones of any team? They just come preprogrammed in the family startup. Entitlement has long come from a birth right. That has been a fundamental principle for almost every culture known to mankind. It is instinctive. But is it any different from any other startup community. I don't think so. If any individual plays a role in the gestation and birth of a business he or she feels entitled. Early team members like family members often fail to keep pace with the business. Often they are overcompensated as a reward for being first in. Resentment happens as new more talented players join the team. Are these not the same issues we've discussed regarding family jealousy and entitlement? Succession is really just one version of the end game and today the end comes sooner for most companies. As long as the speed of change remains dramatic and big business needs to grow through acquisition the scales are loaded in favour of a sale, not a dynasty.

"So the problems are generally the same, just modified, as they are by any adjective, whether lifestyle, female, senior, emerging market, technology, or any other type of entrepreneur we might choose. Every form of entrepreneurship has value. We should analyze the idiosyncrasies and challenges of all types if we want to facilitate and encourage at all levels as I do. As we have seen and you have lived, the solutions can be more complicated for families. Communication can be compromised. Loyalty can impact on the willingness to take action, but the route to the solution lies in understanding the issue and the implications of the problem. None of this changes the reality that family enterprise provides the mainstream entrée to the world of an entrepreneur, either directly or through the creation of a domestic culture of success or by removing barriers and creating opportunity. As long as the family unit is the principal organism of our social structure this will not change, and as long as the human factor enters into decision-making, favouritism, duty, loyalty, entitlement, and judgement will impact the decisions and result in less than optimum results. These are essential elements of the human condition as are greed and fear, which drive behaviour and determine the economic cycle."

The sermon was complete. For me the topic was exhausted. My personal issue had moved toward resolution. Sam had taught me more about myself and my opportunities. The process was worthwhile. I had made new friends, valuable contacts, and maybe found a new job.

Before we could leave Sam called us to attention for the last time.

"Tim and I have a small gift for each of you to thank you for your contribution and to remind you of where you came from and where so many others will get their start. Thank you all, and do watch my Twitter feed. Some brilliant thoughts are on the horizon."

Tim came around handing each of us a parcel. Donna and I exchanged glances and then tore our packages open at once. We each received a beautiful set of stemless wine glasses, four for red and four for white. On each glass was engraved a lightning bolt and the phrase "The Power of Family Unity." I guess the lightning bolt symbolized the unstoppable, explosive, raw power that family entrepreneurship can generate.

That seemed the perfect note to end on.

CHAPTER TWENTY-FIVE

The Good Bye Girls

If you've ever been to summer camp you know that the exodus comes fast and furious; imagine if all the campers had their own wheels. Sam, Tim, Steve, and Peter walked out and left just as fast. Symbolic kisses and hugs were exchanged, but they were all gone in a flash. Mike was staying behind to clean up over the weekend so Donna and I had a last latte with him. Neither of us was in a hurry. It was barely noon and I had no plans for the rest of the day. At first she tried to talk me into a repeat performance of the previous weekend, but I needed to get home. At last she brought up her offer. I wasn't sure if she was serious or had been bluffing for effect to startle my brothers. It was real.

"Mary, if you can't come today, let's set a dinner meeting for next week. The girls and I discussed it last night. Obviously I didn't expect them yesterday, but I'd already spoken to both of them about you. You see, I didn't plan it but last week turned into a bit of an interview and you passed with flying colours. We all want you as our new COO, chief of operations. I know that you're a driver, a person that can make things happen even when they shouldn't be possible. That's a missing ingredient for us. The three of us are too much alike, maybe a little too much in love with the product or the project and not quite as much with the process the way I know you are. Meet us next week and I'll have a formal offer for you, and there will be share options. I want you as a partner."

Mike had overhead but he withdrew to let us talk in private. Tears of gratitude were streaming down my face. Recognition was good for the soul.

"Donna, I thought you were putting on a show for my brothers. I don't know how to react. Of course I'm very interested but I do have to see what they offer as well. I've poured my heart and soul into that business. I think I may be ready to leave, but I need to know all the answers and I need to think it through carefully."

Donna was smiling. "I knew you didn't think I was serious. That's why I needed to talk to you before we left. I couldn't leave you up in the air like that. The girls loved what you did last week on the sample shipment. More importantly, we all felt a connection. No offense meant, but plumbing doesn't cut it compared to fashion. I know it's more stable, but stability isn't exciting. There'll be some travel, some trade shows. I promise it won't be boring and it will be rewarding. I won't overstate it right now, just tell me that you can meet next week with me and the girls and then we can lay out the whole program. Can we do that?"

"Of course Donna. How about Wednesday? Do you want to meet at your office around 4:30?"

That's how it was left. As I was driving home on another beautiful Indian summer day with the sun shining, I remembered that day two weeks before when it was pouring rain. It was hard to ignore the symbolism. I remembered Sam's advice: "Don't sell yourself short." Two weeks earlier I had been a frustrated employee with entrepreneurial ambitions. That day driving back home, I knew for the first time that I was becoming a legitimate entrepreneur. I just didn't know where.

EPILOGUE

November 1, 2014

A year has passed since Sam pulled our group together. Tim has arranged for a reunion this weekend at the inn, but we have stayed in touch. The last time we saw each other was when Mike Reynolds graduated from the MBA program at the Rotman School of Management back in June. Tim arranged that party as well. Everyone loved Mike.

An awful lot of changes emanated from those two weeks spent together. Decisions have been made and in the process the four of us have taken turns serving as a sounding board for the others. Surprisingly Tim Davidson did get permission from all of us to use the recorded program with a few edits as a teaching video. One segment went viral on YouTube. Apparently the day that I called out Jeff Michaels and exposed Peter Charo appealed to a large number of viewers — literally over a million so far. That little confrontation has made me somewhat of an online celebrity. I have more Twitter followers than Sam.

Peter's social media platform continues to sign up subscribers at a phenomenal rate. He and his father Jeffrey are on great terms now. Peter has set up trust funds to finance businesses for his sister Lauren and his brother Jake. The executors are Peter and his father. The terms of the trust require approval from the two trustees for a business proposal before any funds are released. Lauren has become great friends with Monica Simmonds and is currently studying at the Fashion Institute in New York City. Jake is in his second year of engineering and may yet follow a similar career path to his older brother. There is peace within the Charo family.

That's not the case with Steve Jacobi, who walked away from the family business. His sister Paula wouldn't bend, even with pressure asserted by her husband. Steve has moved into the redevelopment business and owns two significant older stone building blocks west of the city, one of which just received draft plan approval. He also has an option on the Speyside Inn and has been pursuing the conversion of those buildings into lofts. His brother-in-law Dave is running the distribution side of the family business still focused on imports from India, but Paula has reduced her hours in the pharmacy and works two days a week on the fabrication division, even bringing in some new high-quality stones from Italy. The company is doing well. As one of two 50 percent owners Steve has little leverage but is trying to force his sister to consider a sale. If only their father's will had left them the flexibility for one to buy out the other. Unfortunately Steve is not speaking to Paula, other than through his lawyer.

Donna has hired a full-time accountant to serve as CFO. Her business has taken off even more with their penetration of the retail market, including adding two more chain stores. Her new chief operations officer has done a brilliant job of improving logistics for the company and implementing the inventory management system designed by the new CFO. The meeting we had on her offer that Wednesday last November went extremely well. The stock options and the remuneration were beyond my dreams. Donna made me an offer that was impossible to refuse. But I did.

The meeting that I had the day before with my brothers went equally well. Ted and Tommy knocked themselves out by offering a new title, a substantial raise, and an offer of a 25 percent equity position in the company. Donna had scared the hell out of them. The idea that I was meeting her the next day cinched it. They held nothing back. Loyalty and duty along with my commitment of the previous five years dictated that I accept. They made me an offer that I couldn't refuse, but I did.

You see, the meeting that I had on the Monday was spectacular. My friend Bruce Hutchison had an offer that was beyond my comprehension. Bruce gave me 100 percent of the common shares of his company. We crystallized maybe 60 percent of his equity value into preferred shares that along with his savings would provide for his retirement. I would have gone farther than that, but Bruce wouldn't hear of it. Bruce saw in me what no one else recognized. I needed to be an entrepreneur. I wanted to be an entrepreneur. But most importantly I would succeed as an entrepreneur. I became Bruce's succession plan. The daughter he never had. The protégé he desperately needed. Bruce became my mentor. When I asked him why he would ever make me such an offer he replied in words that I will never forget.

"I learned long ago that good people can make a bad idea a success while the wrong people can make the best idea fail. You are one of the right people." That sentiment echoed something that Sam said quite often.

With Bruce's blessing I changed the name of the company from Hutchison Plumbing Supplies to Stanza da Bagno, which means bathroom in Italian. You see, I went to Italy with Paula. I wanted to assess what opportunities might come out of the new free trade agreement with the European Union. I needed to get ahead of the curve. I found some likeminded Italian entrepreneurs hoping to expand their market. Now our customers just call us The Stanza. We've added a high-end group of bathroom products from Italy to the products carried by Bruce out of Asia. As Sam said, they have great designs. It's changed our image. We're selling a lot of product for high-end loft conversions and condos in the downtown city core. Surprisingly the basic business has strengthened as well. I've spent a lot of time on logistics and analytics to allow us to manage our inventory and cash flow. We have cut our delivery times from Asia in half and we have become much better at stocking what sells.

In the past year I've also been to China twice, strengthening supply relationships. My knowledge of plumbing from the inside out has allowed me to make Bruce's medium-sized plumbing supply house the principal supplier for three major plumbing firms in the area, doubling our sales volume in the process. Of course we still retain the O'Brien brothers' business. I would never have arrived where I am today without the chances I had to learn within that family business. My company operates with a small board of directors that serve as the best advisory board I could imagine. I sit on the board as the president and CEO. The other two members are outsiders: Bruce Hutchison, former owner with a wealth of experience in the industry, and Sam Macleod, the man who would not let me sell myself short.

APPENDIX I

The Return of the Curve

Sam's theory regarding the distribution of entrepreneurial skills and traits:

1. Everyone has some element of entrepreneurial skills, from zero to hero.
2. The percent of the population with each skill level can be plotted onto a normal distribution represented by a bell curve.
3. The peak of the curve is the average skill level — 50 percent of the population on each side.
4. Those on the left side possess less than average entrepreneurial aptitude.
5. Those on the extreme left have virtually no such skills.
6. Those on the right side possess more than average entrepreneurial aptitude.
7. Those on the extreme right possess the genius we celebrate, like Edison or Jobs.
8. The application of these skills is thwarted by a wide range of obstacles.
9. The world economy is only utilizing a small percent of the total entrepreneurial skills available due to the limitations of culture, education, gender bias, etc.

10. The whole curve can shift to the right through education.
11. Governments are the key to removing these social barriers over time.
12. Government tends to be staffed by people on the left side. There needs to be a change in culture by introducing disruptors to challenge the status quo.
13. Those that fall on the right side of the curve are the key to solving localized economic problems particularly structural employments issues and job creation whereas big business will look elsewhere pursuing competitive advantages that aren't available to small independent business.

One of the main pieces of evidence in support of Sam's premise is the North American experience. We still have too many barriers here. They are maybe not as severe as they once were, but there is still too much talent being denied opportunity. However, it's no accident that there has been a parade of people here from other countries over the past two hundred years. Major cultural and social issues have been recognized here and at least partially dealt with, opening up opportunities not available elsewhere. The more we remove these limitations, the more that can be accomplished through the efforts of entrepreneurs working in concert with a government determined to provide essential services on an efficient basis. We are the experiment that proves the conclusion. Entrepreneurship thrives here like nowhere else. However, the reduction of obstacles that has happened here has been largely accomplished at the hands of an inefficient government. There is more to be done on all fronts. The experiment is still in progress. Entrepreneurship can only achieve optimum results in a free and stable society. Government is the only institution that can guarantee that freedom and provide the stability and infrastructure required for that success. To do this on an affordable, sustainable basis government has to adopt practices from the private sector.

APPENDIX II

Sam's Second Set of Curves:
Trends for The Supply and Demand of Labour

**Why the Ability to Create and Manage Your Own Career
Is Becoming More Critical**

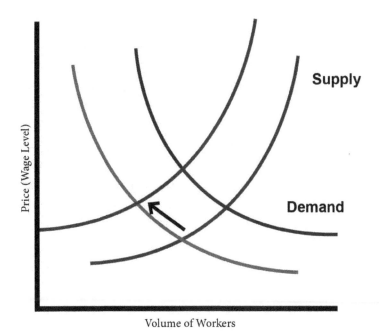

The impact of globalization is to increase the supply of labour in the market, which is represented in the graph by shifting the supply curve to the right — more supply available at every price level. You can see that this shift in supply alone reduces the effective wage rate but increases the number of employed workers.

The impact of technology is to bring about more mechanization and greater efficiency, which reduces the demand for labour. There is less need for labour to achieve the same results. This is represented by shifting the demand curve to the left. On its own, this shift in demand has the impact of reducing the effective wage rate and reducing the number of employed workers.

When you combine the two shifts together you have a much larger potential work force but still fewer workers employed and those that are at the lowest wage equilibrium shown on the graph. This is the trend going on in the world today and it is likely to persist for some time. The two dominant factors, globalization and technology are producing a world entrenched in rapid change. In the process wage levels are being suppressed while those at the top are receiving huge bonuses. As a result of these factors, job stability is disappearing, the distribution of wealth is skewed in favour of the super-rich and upward mobility for the individual is in decline. Individuals in the West are the most vulnerable to a downward trend in real wage rates.

By becoming an entrepreneur an individual effectively controls the demand for his own labour and also captures the value added for the service or product he or she provides. In the process they also create jobs and opportunities for others. If you don't choose to be an employer, than managing your own career effectively in an entrepreneurial fashion will increase the demand for your specific labour and provide the opportunity for upward mobility and higher rewards in the form of wages.

APPENDIX III

Sam's Tweets

1. Having ideas makes you a dreamer. Making those ideas happen converts you to an entrepreneur.
2. A plan is one possible outcome. The planning process provides a framework to anticipate and adjust.
3. Entrepreneurship is a life philosophy grounded in opportunity, fuelled by determination, and focused on results.
4. Growth is the life's blood for most entrepreneurs but it can act like a python, exhausting your strengths and crushing your ability to survive.
5. Innovation is not entrepreneurship. For every innovation there are thousands of entrepreneurs who will find applications.
6. We only fail when we give up. Setbacks are part of the learning curve on the road to success.
7. Entrepreneurs love the process more than the project. Innovators exist for the project.
8. A successful entrepreneur relies on managed risk and measured success while avoiding reckless risk and failure.
9. There can only be one business that does something first. Finding ways to do it better and different adds many more paths to success.

10. Worry is counterproductive. If it happens you've endured it twice. If it doesn't you've wasted time and energy worrying for nothing.

11. Failure is overrated. Learn from it if you must. Avoid it if you can.

12. Entrepreneurship takes many forms. The common bonds are the personal issues faced and the fundamental business challenges mastered.

13. Startup reality check: your project will take twice as long, cost twice as much, and yield half the profit that you expect.

14. Self-deception creates a path to failure. An open mind molds the key to success.

15. Anticipation paves the road to solutions while preoccupation creates a roadblock to success.

16. Doubt is the forerunner of indecision. Confidence is the breeding ground for achievement.

17. If a problem can be solved with money it is not a problem.

18. The learning curve of an entrepreneur is forged from mistakes and setbacks as well as triumphs and accomplishments.

19. Easy is the twin of lazy.

20. Difficult is the cousin of determination.

21. Mediocre is the brother of excuse.

22. Success is the sister of effort.

23. Defeat is a setback. Retreat is a retrenchment. Only surrender is a failure.

24. Entrepreneurship depends on managing risk, not just taking it.

25. Pick your team to fly high and fly low relating to your entire staff.

26. There is a fine line between self-confidence and arrogance.

27. In the era of big data, how much of what we know do we understand?

28. If you're lucky enough to be an entrepreneur, then you're lucky enough.

29. Beware of the sense of entrepreneurial infallibility.

30. If necessity is the mother of invention then opportunity is the father of entrepreneurship.

31. Globalization rewards small, flexible, and adaptable business focusing on economies of scale and the law of diminishing returns.

32. Entrepreneurs love the process, with the best part being you can do it again and again.

33. Focus on what you love while making sure you do the things that you hate.

34. In a quantum world there are no limitations.

35. Entrepreneurs define their world as quantum.

36. Entrepreneurship is an economic catalyst — the economic resource that puts all other resources to work.

37. Entrepreneurs love the process more than the project, the challenge more than the reward, and the solution above all.

38. Opportunity is the father of entrepreneurship, but determination is the cornerstone of success.

39. Entrepreneurship isn't a spectator sport. Teamwork is critical. The bench is thin. The coaches play.

40. If religion is the opiate of the masses, then optimism is the drug of choice for entrepreneurs.

41. Entrepreneurs exist in a revolving door of problem solving. Enjoy the ride. Ask questions and listen.

42. Don't neglect your most valuable asset. Pay yourself, take vacations, and find balance.

43. Indecision undermines leadership.

44. Being decisive inspires confidence.

45. Problems and complaints are the prime source of improvement.

46. Every problem is an opportunity. Every solution brings a reward.

47. Entrepreneurs are like the forwards in hockey, they dig in the corners and make things happen.
48. Every idea is not an opportunity.
49. Entrepreneurs change the world, and right now the world needs changing.
50. Entrepreneurship is a life philosophy sustained by determination.
51. Failure sucks! Learn from it when it happens. Prevent it if you can.
52. Fears are normal. Harness them to succeed.
53. One of the strongest motivations is the fear of failure.
54. The lean startup isn't new. Controlling costs and testing the market have always been prudent.
55. Fears are warnings helping you to anticipate. Embrace them to succeed. Deny them to fail.
56. Making sales at the expense of margin is like a dog chasing its tail. There is no fool like a busy fool.
57. We are a world in transition. Entrepreneurs must make contacts in emerging markets.
58. Park your ego. Trust your team. Being wrong happens. Admitting it does not make you weak.
59. A questioning mind is the source of many opportunities.
60. No one minds if you make a mistake. No one remembers once you fix it.
61. Entrepreneurs are jugglers, dealing with one thing but having several others on their radar.
62. Don't sacrifice your team culture through neglect.
63. People rarely change. If someone doesn't fit your team, every member knows it.
64. A career as an entrepreneur is like running the gauntlet. Everyone wants a piece of you, but the run is glorious.
65. Life is an evolving path leading to opportunities, but it takes a certain mindset to see them.
66. The most important skill you can master today is the

ability to create and manage your own career.

67. The right people can make a bad idea a success.
68. The wrong people will make the best idea fail.
69. Disruption challenges the status quo, leading to innovation.
70. Entrepreneurs are disruptors.
71. It is creative destruction that renews capitalism.
72. Entrepreneurs are problem solvers. The bigger the problem, the bigger the reward.
73. We are entering a new age of entrepreneurship.
74. Too big to fail really means too big to succeed.
75. Entrepreneurs have never been more important.
76. Every family business has a full cast of characters, both drivers and passengers.
77. Family loyalty can become an obsession just one step away from delusion.
78. One of the principal barriers to entrepreneurship is prison thinking.
79. Family ties can bind you, but family support can launch your success.
80. Simply being able to do something is a poor excuse for doing it.
81. The essence of consulting is finding multiple employers.
82. Creativity does not ensure viability.
83. The most painful result is becoming a creative success but a financial failure.
84. Technology is reducing the demand for labour.
85. Globalization is increasing the supply of available labour.
86. There is downward pressure on the price paid for labour in the form of real wages.
87. The middle class in the West is under downward pressure as real wages decline.
88. Job stability is disappearing in the face of global competition.

89. There is an increasing discrepancy in the distribution of wealth favouring the rich.
90. Employer expectations are increasing, focused on 24/7 availability.
91. Becoming an entrepreneur allows you to employ and capitalize on your own labour.
92. Becoming entrepreneurial allows you to manage and control your career.
93. Empathy is the key to understanding other's problems, which leads to meaningful opportunities.
94. Family obligations can cloud judgement in the face of difficult decisions.
95. There will be thousands of independent businesses seeking successors within the next ten years.
96. The retirement plan for many baby boomers hinges on the sale of their business.
97. The marriage of a niche-established businesses with up to date technology is a great opportunity.
98. There will soon be many businesses available that can be acquired on an earn-out basis
99. Toxic relationships in a family business can sink a stable ship.
100. Never underestimate the determination and resilience of a CEO responsible for the family brand.

IN THE SAME SERIES

Everyday Entrepreneur

Making It Happen

The Entrepreneurial Edge

Fred Dawkins

"The most important skill in the 21st century will be the ability to create your own job."

In *Everyday Entrepreneur*, you will meet three individuals who all have entrepreneurial aspirations. The first is Tim, whose career is stagnating, despite having a good job. Tim has developed some software that could form the basis of his own business, but he can't make the decision whether or not to set up on his own. Terry, a childhood friend, steers Tim into a class on entrepreneurship conducted by a mysterious person named Sam. The class includes two others: Grace, in her mid-thirties, and Mike, who is twenty-something. Sam invites his three students to learn to become entrepreneurs over a period of twelve days. By focusing on the qualities of a successful entrepreneur and by relying on a wide range of anecdotes, he cleverly leads all three to make important decisions about their future.

Fred Dawkins's practical insights and advice can help you identify your own strengths and empower you to take the leap to an entrepreneur — and make your dream a reality.

PRAISE FOR
Everyday Entrepreneur

"Fred Dawkins has written a wonderful book about entrepreneurship unlike any other on the market. He brilliantly uses his storytelling skills to illuminate his subject in a way that makes the book a joy to read. You're so wrapped up in the story that you may not realize how much you're learning until you've turned that last page."
— Terry Fallis, award-winning author of *The Best Laid Plans* and *Up and Down*.

"*Everyday Entrepreneur* offers a simple but effective road map anyone can use to take the fear out of following your entrepreneurial dreams."
— Monica Mehta, award-winning author of *The Entrepreneurial Instinct* and *INC Magazine* columnist.

"Fred Dawkins employs a likeable cast of characters and the simple setting of Canadian cottage country in July to convey a complex set of ideas ranging from the nature-versus-nurture debate (are entrepreneurs born or made?) to a variety of essential how-to entrepreneurship skills to specialty topics such as gender, leadership, negotiation, and team formation, as well as the important role of entrepreneurship in the global economy. His casual, easy-to-read writing style belies the critical importance of his subject matter. Not just potential entrepreneurs but also governments, big companies, and business schools in the West must adapt to the new reality of an increasingly educated and ambitious middle class in so-called developing countries and take immediate steps to reinvigorate

"The analyses of factors dominating business and society are insightful and demonstrative. Fred Dawkins has a wonderful capacity to put things in perspective, a writing style that is captivating and his command of the English language speaks for itself. I believe this will make a great college text book since it would inspire great discussions — arguments? I'd love to be teaching from it. Also a great question and answer book for would-be entrepreneurs."

— Dr. Freeman McEwen, Dean Emeritus, University of Guelph.

"Wonderfully scribed. [The] story is easy to read, compelling, and worthy of a broad spectrum of society. As I got deeper into it, despite the undocumented postulates of Sam's theories, the story continuously got more intense while spinning of increasingly important concepts required of any entrepreneurial undertaking. Sam's ideas ring with the sounds of truth, wisdom, and familiar experiences. I loved it."

— Marvin Barnett, president, Finer Space Corporation, serial entrepreneur of over forty years.

"I worked with Fred during the negotiations of a first collective agreement for his business which was growing rapidly. His understanding of the issues and his coolness in what many would describe as high pressure moments contributed to his ultimate success and control of the situation. Before you quit your job to set up your own business or hire an accountant or do your due diligence you should read this book."

— Steven F. Wilson, partner, Mathews, Dinsdale & Clark LLP.

our large population of underutilized problem-solvers in order to remain competitive and continue to enjoy increasing prosperity. As Sam would say: It is not a question of if, but rather how."

— Ajay Agrawal, Peter Munk Professor of Entrepreneurship at the University of Toronto's Rotman School of Management, founder of the Creative Destruction Lab for entrepreneurs, and co-founder of The Next 36 entrepreneurship program.

"Technology entrepreneurs all too often focus only on different ways of acquiring customers, equity value, and raising venture capital money. What is lost in the discussion is all the human issues you will face as you build your business. Fred Dawkins offers a perspective that I think is missing in the current international discussion around entrepreneurship and one that I think founders of technology companies need to consider at an early stage."

— Jesse Rodgers, director of the Creative Destruction Lab at the University of Toronto, builder of VeloCity at the University of Waterloo, and co-founder of Tribehr.com.

"I just finished reading [this] book and enjoyed it immensely. [Fred has] pulled together a wealth of knowledge and advice crucial to the successful entrepreneur in a highly readable fashion. It is a must-read for aspiring and seasoned entrepreneurs who are facing today's complex, volatile, and uncertain world. I especially appreciate the emphasis on thinking globally and adapting proactively. We have seen too many examples of yesterday's winner relying on old models to their detriment. It isn't easy ... but it is exciting and gratifying to create your own business and work to see it flourish. The summary at the end of the book should be bookmarked on every entrepreneur's computer."

— Dr. Sherry Cooper, former executive VP and chief economist for BMO and author of three books, including *The New Retirement: How it Will Change Our Future.*